Hubie [illegible] prophet and a friend. You too will n[illegible] and unpacks this genuine gift.

—Sid Roth
Host, *It's Supernatural!*

This book is a compelling story of a man who did not let his past or life's detours keep him from allowing the Lord to speak through him declaring significant and life-changing prophecies. You will not want to put this book down as you become a part of Hubie Synn's struggles, triumphs, and amazing encounters.

—Joni Lamb
Cofounder, Daystar Television Network

This is an amazing, true-life story of an accountant who has become a prophet and now sees miracles follow him almost everywhere he goes. I know him personally as well as many of those whose lives he has touched with the supernatural gift that is working in his life.

My dear friend Rabbi Jonathan Cahn was thrust into Hubie's world of supernatural prophetic gifts while sitting in the Charlotte airport. Later Rabbi Cahn became a *New York Times* best-selling author.

Who would ever have believed that a certified public account would tell New York Giants football player David Tyree that he would make a catch that would elevate him to a world stage. That catch is now known in Super Bowl history as one of the greatest catches of all time!

These two stories are just the beginning of the amazing book *The Tales of a Wandering Prophet.*

I have seen Hubie walk into a crowded room and then leave after personally touching hundreds of people with a word from God. I am an eyewitness to the wandering prophet, and I recommend this book!

—Jim Bakker
Host, *The Jim Bakker Show*

Hubie Synn has a powerful prophetic gift that has been a great blessing to me personally as well as my ministry. One of the most important narratives of this book is the fact that Hubie can obey the prophetic call of God upon his life while still functioning in the marketplace. This book will give faith, hope, and courage to all believers, and show how anyone who loves Jesus can have a profound impact upon this world!

—Bishop Joseph Mattera

Presiding Bishop, Christ Covenant Coalition

Overseeing Bishop, Resurrection Church, New York

Hubie Synn is the real deal—a genuine, certified, real-life prophet. I know because he has told me things about my life he could not possibly have known except through the leading of the Holy Spirit. Likewise, his book is the real deal—breezy, compelling, satisfying, persuasive, and inspiring. I read it in two hours that seemed like ten minutes. While it delivered the goods, I kept looking for more. I can't wait for the sequel.

—Joseph Farah

Editor and chief executive officer, WND.com

Hubie Synn's charming and self-effacing book takes you inside the head of the reluctant prophet—arguing with God and timidly approaching complete strangers to tell them, "God has a word for you." It is utterly fascinating.

—Squire Rushnell

New York Times Best-Selling Author

When God Winks Books

Hubie Synn, the shy accountant with an amazing prophetic gift, proves that God uses the most unlikely people to do His work. This book is funny, compelling, and powerful. I couldn't put it down!

—Louise DuArt

Author, *Godwink Stories* and *Couples Who Pray*

Comedic Impressionist

Having lived through the abuses of the prophetic in the body of Christ over the past few decades, there is no way anyone could have convinced me that I would be endorsing a book on the subject. I've known Hubie and Vicki Synn for over twenty years. I've watched them grow as a family and in God's graces. Seeing how, with such humility, Hubie has accepted and is walking in his prophetic calling restores my faith in the church's ability to use this gift properly. We desperately need to see all of the gifts in operation but only when motivated by pure hearts. This book is refreshing, funny, touching, daunting, but most of all honest.

—Charles Bernard "CB" Murray 4th
Pastor and Executive Board Member
Kingdom Churches Worldwide
Writer, Producer, and Composer, Euphonixs Inc.

Few people find unique expression of ministry in and through their lives as Hubie Synn has done. His extraordinary discernment has blessed people such as David Tyree and Jonathan Cahn to encourage them in ministry outreach, publication, and to stand for Christ in our world today. Reading this extraordinary work will encourage the reader that a living God is at work in and through His "children."

—Tom Phillips
Vice President, Billy Graham Library

My wife, Annie, and I have known Hubie Synn and his wife, Vicki, for over twenty years now. In that time we've participated together in worship and fund-raisers, ran the New York City Marathon, ministered alongside both of them, watched them raise their five beautiful children, and cooked and eaten lots of great meals together. In that time the example of humility and Christ-centeredness and the word in Hubie's mouth have continued to inspire and encourage not only my family but also the thousands of lives Hubie has touched and continues to touch.

—John Cavazos
Senior Pastor, Christ the King Church
Kissimmee, Florida

In this book Hubie shares his experience with God that is relevant to us today. His encounter with God and obedience to

His voice has caused him to be one of the clear and trusted prophetic voices today. Hubie is also one of the most accurate prophetic voices I have ever heard in my twenty-six years of ministry.

—Frankie Rathanum
Senior Pastor and Founder, Tower of Faith Ministries
British Virgin Islands

Prophets are there to foretell the future, whether they are prophesying the most amazing catch in Super Bowl history or keeping someone on track with their mission to change the world for the better. We all need a little encouragement sometimes to stay the course and hold fast to what God has put in our hearts to do.

Hubie has been just that voice to me and the many he has prophesied to. I met Hubie in a strange but impactful way that revealed his gift at a time when I needed to hear from God to be encouraged. Hubie had so specifically and accurately prophesied about my friend Patty and me in an e-mail to an associate of ours that it got his wife's attention, and she reached out to me to discover if Hubie secretly knew us or about us. That is when she had me read Hubie's prophecy about Patty and me and our involvement in her husband's life. We assured her that we had never met Hubie or knew anything about him, and he knew nothing about us. Our curiosity piqued, we decided to fly across country from California to New York to meet Hubie face-to-face.

Hubie hears from God, and those of us who have benefited from that connection are very grateful! Now you can all read about his adventures.

—Daryn Hinton
Author, artist manager, and TV and film producer

THE TALES OF A *Wandering* PROPHET

HUBIE SYNN

CHARISMA HOUSE

Most Charisma House Book Group products are available at special quantity discounts for bulk purchase for sales promotions, premiums, fund-raising, and educational needs. For details, write Charisma House Book Group, 600 Rinehart Road, Lake Mary, Florida 32746, or telephone (407) 333-0600.

Tales of a Wandering Prophet by Hubie Synn
Published by Charisma House
Charisma Media/Charisma House Book Group
600 Rinehart Road
Lake Mary, Florida 32746
www.charismahouse.com

Some names, places, and identifying details with regard to stories in this book have been changed to help protect the privacy of individuals who may have been involved or had similar experiences.

Cover design by Justin Evans

Visit the author's website at www.pursuehimministries.org.

Library of Congress Cataloging-in-Publication Data:
Synn, Hubie.
The tales of a wandering prophet / by Hubie Synn. -- First edition.
pages cm
ISBN 978-1-62136-982-0 (trade paper) -- ISBN 978-1-62136-983-7 (e-book)
1. Synn, Hubie. 2. Evangelists--United States--Biography. 3. Prophecy--Christianity. I. Title.
BV3785.S96A3 2015
269'.2092--dc23
[B]

2015007567

15 16 17 18 19 — 98765432
Printed in the United States of America

CONTENTS

ACKNOWLEDGMENTS

WITHOUT THE FOLLOWING people, this book would not have been possible. I would like to thank:

Jesus, my Lord and Savior, for saving me and for being patient with me!

My loving wife, Vicki, who has stood me by me while the Lord molded and shaped me. It has been a process, but you clung to me while it was all happening and made sure we did it together!

My children. Sara, Daniel, Kristin, Paul, and Michael, for your understanding, patience, and support. You mean the world to me, and I am grateful to be your father!

Steve and Joy Strang, for giving me this opportunity.

The Charisma House team, especially Tessie DeVore, Woodley Auguste, Debbie Marrie, Adrienne Gaines, Marcos Perez, and Joel Kilpatrick.

Miriam Webster, for your songs that encouraged us and gave us hope during times of trial.

Special thanks to: Prudence Lo, Eric Hussey, Helen Teike, Tanya Jones, CB Murray, Walter Iwanciw, Coco Mitchell, Lucy Wang, Squire Rushnell, Louise DuArt, Glacia Robinson, Norah Harper, Cherry Williams, Elise

Wims, Sheri Tennant, David Ramirez, Daryn Hinton, Patty Gannon, Darius Young, Wendy Mitchell, Maryrose Marrale, Michael Devalera, John Longman, Stryper, and Switchfoot.

And last, I would like to express my deep gratitude to these wonderful families: the Cruzes, Matteras, Cahns, Shahids, Tyrees, Jamisons, Millses, McLemores, Thompsons, Colletons, Rathanums, Sepes, Happles, Eppersons, Schweisthals, Onyias, Los, Husseys, Goldsteins, Ahluwalias, Raises, Repaldos, Rifkins, Goldsholles, Rosens, Kirschenbaums, Rands, Sollies, Liuzzas, Chois, Moels, Neals, Barbaricks, Reins, Lees, Shirleys, Dashers, Draperses, Wollschlagers, Ferries, De Merses, Milos, McClouds, Bowdens, and Changs.

FOREWORD

I NEVER WRITE FOREWORDS. It's not that I'm not asked. I am, continuously. The problem is that I haven't had a moment to write a foreword, much less the time to read the books sent to me. But this is one case where it was impossible to decline. If it wasn't for Hubie Synn, *The Harbinger* would not have gone forth to America—at least not in the way it did.

It all began in an airport in Charlotte, North Carolina. It was there that a meeting took place that neither of us planned but that would change both of our lives and the lives of people across the world.

I had just finished writing *The Harbinger.* I had no idea how it would be published. I had never written a book before, and the chances of this one finding a publisher were small to next to nothing. I only knew it was of the Lord. That same week I was flying out to Dallas, Texas, to speak at a Promise Keepers gathering. The plane stopped in Charlotte. I headed to the gate to catch the next plane and sat down by the window. I was exhausted. The previous night I had preached at the Friday evening service at Beth Israel, the congregation I lead. The flight schedule required me to be at the airport at 3:00 a.m. I would preach again in Dallas that day having had no sleep.

Except for the fact that I had given my word, I would have traded it all for a warm bed. Yet as I sat on the airport bench, I felt an urgency to commit the going forth of *The Harbinger* into the Lord's hands. I bowed my head and prayed that the Lord would send forth the message in the form of a book not by the plans or hands of men, but by His own hand.

I opened my eyes. There was a man sitting to my left. He wasn't there before. "What's the good word?" he asked. I took him for a businessman and his question to be the kind of casual, non-serious remark one might expect from someone sitting at a bar. Little did I know that it was just an excuse to deliver a prophetic message.

I answered him. We began making small talk. We discovered that the other was a believer, but not much more. Then they announced my flight. Before I could board the plane, he told me I had to wait. He had a word to give me. He began speaking. The words concerned the future, what God was about to do. In the process he handed me a hundred dollars as a sign that the Lord would greatly multiply the ministry He had given me.

The words rang true to the point that once we were on the plane, I asked him to repeat them. I grabbed the notebook I had taken with me in which were the pages of the message I was to give in Dallas. Then I began jotting down, rapid fire, the words as he spoke them. Everything he told me that day would come true, and that very encounter would prove instrumental in its coming true. It was that meeting that would cause *The Harbinger* to go forth to America and the world. And it would happen not by literary agents nor by any natural means, but by the hand of God—just as I had prayed it would. The encounter was the very answer to the prayer I had just offered up, the fastest answer to any prayer I had ever witnessed, happening just seconds after I finished praying it.

For those who don't believe that God can do such things, the pages of the Bible are filled with them—prophetic encounters, moments, and words. For those who don't believe God can *still* do such things today, I would say it is never a wise thing to tell God what He can and cannot still do. He is free to do as He chooses to do. And the fact is, it happened. Whenever you see a copy of *The Harbinger*, it is, aside from everything else, a testimony bearing witness to that prophetic encounter.

My relationship with Hubie didn't end there at that airport. Since that time I've come to know him as a friend. I can bear witness that he is a man of sincerity, integrity, humility, gentleness, compassion, truth, and godliness. And he is unlikely. If you had to pick the man who gave such prophetic words in a lineup of suspects, he would be among the last chosen. If there is a type, it isn't him. Rather he is unassuming, an accountant who never trumpets his gift and only uses it as led and to serve others.

It is for this reason that his story is so compelling and his words much more authoritative than those of most self-proclaimed prophets. His is, above all, a story of what God can do with any of us, if we open up our lives to be without reservation for His will and glory. It is a similar story told of the great saints of the Bible, most of whom reacted to their calling with shock and feelings of not being worthy. God does not call the able; He enables the called. Our part is simply to be open, willing, and ready. And if we will be open, willing, and ready, there is no limit and no telling how greatly God can use our lives. Just ask Hubie Synn. And if one day, while sitting at an airport, waiting for your flight, you should notice an unassuming

Asian-looking man sitting nearby, and he should ask you, "What's the good word?" I would definitely answer him—and keep a pen and paper close by...just in case.

RABBI JONATHAN CAHN is the author of the *New York Times* best sellers *The Harbinger* and *The Mystery of the Shemitah* and leader of the Jerusalem Center/Beth Israel in Wayne, New Jersey.

Introduction

PROPHESYING AT THE AIRLINE GATE

I WAS IN NO mood to be used prophetically by God.

Wind and rain were pounding the landscape outside my home in New Jersey. I was supposed to fly to Dallas, but the weather had made a mess of everyone's itineraries. Flights were delayed and canceled, and my own 5:30 p.m. flight was bumped to ten o'clock that night—too late to catch a connecting flight from Charlotte, North Carolina, to my sister's home in Dallas. My sister had been diagnosed with stomach cancer, and every delay meant less time with her in what would perhaps be our last visit together.

The airline rescheduled me for a flight the next morning. My thoughts were swirling, and I didn't sleep that night. Life felt challenging on several fronts—I wasn't enjoying my job, my sister was dying, and now my time with her was shrinking by the hour. "Lord, just get me there," I prayed, feeling the weekend slip away.

Turbulence on the flight made napping impossible, and when we landed in Charlotte, I was in a terrible mood. I went straight to an airport Starbucks, grabbed a large coffee, and headed to the gate to nurse my misery. Weary travelers and storm refugees crowded the gate, and I saw only one seat available—way over by the windows, my least favorite spot. I dragged myself there, plunked down half-willingly, turned on my iPod, and began to sip the coffee. It was time to close my eyes and disappear.

Then it came. Unmistakable—the nudge of the Lord.

"No way," I thought. "I did not just feel that. Forget about it."

A few moments passed and another nudge came, this one stronger. I turned the music in my headphones louder and tried to ignore the urging, but now I was having a very unwelcome conversation with the Lord.

"Really?" I said sourly. "Now? Don't You know how I feel? I am not in the mood for this."

Nudge.

His prodding was so strong that it may as well have been an elbow in my ribs. I reluctantly opened my eyes and glanced around, annoyed, and tried to see what the Lord was drawing my attention to. People were everywhere, standing sentry with their luggage, biding time until boarding.

"There."

To my right was a Jewish-looking man with black, curly hair and a full beard.

"What? He's Jewish," I said silently to the Lord, hoping to dismiss the assignment. I sipped my coffee and tried to settle back into some type of rest.

Nudge.

"You've got to be kidding me."

His prodding was persistent and irritating. I looked at the Jewish man again and spied what he was reading…a small book, the Book of Proverbs.

"Look, it's Old Testament," I said to the Lord, indicating that surely this was not the kind of guy who would receive prophecy from a Christian like me.

Nudge.

"Lord, now is not the time! No, I do not want to do this!" I felt like saying aloud.

In spite of myself, my attention was now glued to the Jewish man. He was slouching in his chair and by all appearances praying.

"Lord, see? He's praying like the Orthodox do at the Western Wall. Surely not this guy."

Nudge.

My stomach began turning, making me feel sick—a sure indicator in my life that I was disobeying the Lord's leading to open my mouth and share a word from Him.

"OK, OK." I relented only because I knew the Lord would not leave me alone and that at some point I'd be sticking my head in a trash can being sick. Away went my headphones; to the floor went my coffee. With one last peaceful breath and expecting the worst, I turned to the Jewish man and said simply, "What's the good word?"

The man looked at me.

"God loves you," he said in a surprisingly confident, resonant voice.

Relief hit me like a warm breeze. But his response also caught me off guard.

"Yes, I know," was all I could think to say.

"You know? You are a believer?" he asked.

"Yes," I said, and we began to chat casually. He was in ministry, he said, and I told him I was in ministry as well—of a sort. After a few minutes of small talk, a crackling announcement came over the speakers that it was time to board the plane. It looked like our conversation would end and be forgotten, like so many thousands of conversations in settings like these. The man started to get up. But I knew this interaction wasn't over yet.

"Wait," I said.

He paused and looked at me questioningly. Though we were both believers, this next step was never easy. No predictable path exists to tell someone, "I have something else to tell you." The stakes always feel high, and embarrassment is a real possibility. But I had to obey. Even on this day, feeling as bad as I did, God had given me an assignment.

"The Lord wants to tell you something," I said, bracing for his response.

"OK," he said and sat back down. His face betrayed no emotion except perhaps caution.

"Here we go," I thought.

Then I did what the Scriptures talk about in Psalm 81:10: "Open your mouth wide, and I will fill it." I opened my mouth and out came a long, detailed word for this man I had just met. As usual, I felt the words coming out of me but had no knowledge of what I was saying before I said it. I usually didn't even get the benefit of listening to what I was saying but rather functioned as the conduit for God's words to flow. I hoped the man was hearing them and getting their full meaning, because I sure wasn't.

When I finally stopped, the man looked at me in silence. With nothing else to say, I just looked back at him. It felt scary. "What is he going to do?" I thought. "Scoff at me and walk away? Inform the airline that there's a troublesome passenger on this flight who may accost other passengers? What happens next?"

"You are aboard this flight, right?" he asked me.

"Yes," I said.

"When we go up in the air, I am going to come and find you," he said.

"Find me? Why?"

"What you just said is very important, and you don't realize what it means."

"You're right. I have no idea what I said," I told him.

"You have to tell me the word again. It is so important."

Now I was in trouble.

"It doesn't work that way," I said, knowing there was no way I could recall the word. It had traveled through my mouth without ever taking residence in my brain. Still, he got up confidently and said, "I am going to come and find you on the flight." He walked toward the boarding line.

I found my seat on the plane, still trying to comprehend the situation. I really didn't like these scenarios. Delivering a word was one thing, but talking with someone about it afterward? Not for me. My job was done, and I had nothing else to say. "Maybe he won't come and look for me," I thought. "How can I bring the word back when I don't even know what I said?"

Worry made an assault on my mind, but I battled back—"It's not my problem. I did what I needed to do, and that's all I need to do. Now I just want to settle in and pick up some lost scraps of sleep."

I reclined my chair but couldn't sleep knowing that this guy might actually come looking for me as he said he would. When the plane reached a cruising altitude, sure enough the Jewish man came walking down the aisle, head bobbing back and forth with excitement. His smile was so wide it practically knocked people out of their seats. I noticed he was armed with a pen and notepad.

"Maybe he'll pass by and not recognize me," I thought futilely.

He stopped right next to my seat.

"Hey, hey, come on. Let's go to the back of the plane," he said excitedly as he made his way down the aisle and hand signaled me to follow.

I dutifully followed, doubting that anything fruitful would come of it. Two seats were available by the galley. He pulled the tray table down, set his notepad on it, and clicked open his pen.

"OK," he said intently, "Tell me again."

I stammered, "It doesn't work that way. When it comes, it just comes. I can't control it. I've got nothing more. I don't even know what I said."

He seemed to understand my explanation, and nodded.

"Let's pray," he said. So we did. To my surprise, while we were praying the word returned. I began to speak it, and he wrote it down, scribbling, flipping the page and scribbling some more.

"Thank You, God!" I said silently.

Then it ended. The man turned to me with resolve. "Don't get offended, but how accurate are you?" he asked.

"As far as I know, very," I said, trying to answer truthfully but without any trace of pride.

He smiled. Then he shared that many parts of the word I had given him were very similar to a word he had received from a guy in South America. As we talked, the plane went through a patch of turbulence.

"We are going to be fine since this word has to come true," the man said, and we both laughed. "Thank you again," he said. "You really have no idea what you have done and how much it means."

"I just did what I needed to do," I said.

Never would I have dreamed that this new friendship would continue, or that millions of readers would soon read a book by this Messianic believer who received a confirming word from God from a stranger in Charlotte.

Even less did I suspect that God intended to use me—a nobody, an accountant, a regular guy—to deliver messages from heaven to people of all kinds, from total strangers to some of the most famous people in the country. In the coming years I would watch the Holy Spirit open doors I would have thought impossible, shoving me through them sometimes against my will.

My life would end up looking nothing like I had planned. But God was determined to use me to speak to people. My job, if I could manage it, was simply to obey.

Chapter 1

SUPER BOWL CATCH

MY FAMILY AND I sat in our living room watching Super Bowl XLII, the New York Giants versus the undefeated New England Patriots. As a Jets fan I normally wouldn't have paid much attention to the game. Like most Americans, I would have enjoyed the commercials, hoped for some good competition, and then moved on with life.

But this Super Bowl was different. God had told us in advance that something special would happen. And my wife, Vicki, and I felt a witness in our spirits that "the moment" was just about to arrive.

Through a series of divinely orchestrated events, months earlier I had given a word from God to one of the New York Giants players. At that point the team's season was going down the tubes, and this particular player was injured and had just undergone surgery. Nothing seemed less likely than the word coming true.

Now we were watching the scrappy Giants give the fearsome Patriots a serious challenge. "What's going to happen, Lord? What will the moment look like? When will it happen?" I kept wondering. We were sure the word would be fulfilled—but we had no idea how or when.

The story had started the previous summer when I gave up a lucrative job as a CFO in the fashion industry in obedience to God. Our finances were suddenly falling short, and I began working as a certified public accountant with a financial advisor in Staten Island. One day the advisor took me to visit one of his clients, a football player.

David Tyree was an All-Pro special teams player for the New York Giants. He also played wide receiver, but was low on the depth chart for that position. He was mostly known in the league as a dangerous punt blocker and gunner, the guy who tries to block the punt or tackle the kick returner when he catches the ball. I had never heard of him until the day I arrived at his house for a meeting. David answered the door, and I could see the stitches from the recent surgery to his injured wrist.

We went inside, and we all sat down at the kitchen table to talk through some financial stuff. David's two kids walked up to me and started to talk to me. "I really don't need to be here," I thought. "I'm not contributing anything to this conversation." At one point toward the end of the meeting the advisor turned to me and said to David, "By the way, this is Hubie. He's a CPA, and he will be doing your taxes from now on."

"OK," David replied, and that was that. The advisor and I said good-bye and headed back to the office. I had spent so little time with David that I didn't even remember what he looked like.

So it was a little strange when a couple of days after our meeting I felt a stirring to pray for David. Why, I didn't know. We were barely acquainted and probably wouldn't have recognized each other on the street. David wasn't even playing football, because of his injury, and it wasn't certain he would play again that season. He was virtually unknown except to Giants fans and die-hard NFL fans. But I felt God pushing me to pray for him.

"OK, he's injured," I thought. "I'll pray for that."

I also prayed for his family, his career, and his life in general, about which I knew little.

"That should do it," I thought, believing the prayer assignment was over.

But over the next few weeks I found myself praying for David often. He kept popping to mind during the workday and when I was relaxing at home. I dutifully prayed for him but couldn't make sense of it given that we had met so briefly.

Then the Holy Spirit began waking me up during the night to pray for David for long periods of time. That got old pretty fast. "Lord, why is this happening?" I thought as my eyes popped open an hour after I had fallen asleep. The only answer was a drumbeat in my head: *Pray for David, pray for David, pray for David.* I prayed in tongues and with my understanding, and fell back asleep, only to wake up again. *You're not done yet. Keep praying. Keep praying for David.*

Never had my sleep been interrupted like that. "This is a little weird," I thought. Not a day went by that I didn't feel an urgency to pray for this man whom I barely knew. David Tyree was very much on God's mind, but I was to the point of wishing He would leave me alone.

"Call Him"

In the meantime, my relationship with the financial advisor wasn't going well. Coming from my previous position as a CFO, I had a lot of confidence and ideas for doing our work better, but the advisor didn't seem interested in my ideas. Time after time I felt my suggestions weren't getting a hearing. "Lord, why am I even here?" I asked in frustration more than once. "Can't You release me from this job? Surely I can find other work. This whole partnership thing isn't going as well as I thought it would."

"Stay," the Lord impressed on me, and I reluctantly obeyed. I continued to work for the advisor but stopped offering suggestions. Whatever the advisor told me to do, I did. But I was asking God if every day could be my last one at this job.

Then one day at the office the Holy Spirit spoke clearly: "You need to call David."

"Call him? I just met him, and it was only for a few minutes," I told the Lord. "We haven't even spoken since that day at his house."

Call him.

"This can't be You, Lord," I thought to myself and pushed the bizarre idea away.

An uneasy, anxious feeling badgered me all day, and I knew the only solution was to obey the perplexing word the Lord had given me. "OK, Lord," I finally said, "if this is You, then I'll do it." I copied David's home number from the office telephone directory onto a sheet of paper and put it in my pocket. The uneasy feeling stopped immediately. "Strange," I thought.

Though I had been walking with the Lord for nearly twenty years, at that time I knew next to nothing about how the spiritual gifts functioned. I had no training and no clear understanding of what prophecy was, and would not have characterized what I was experiencing as a manifestation of one of the gifts. I simply followed where the Lord led and tried to obey what He said. I often felt guided by feelings of urgency, anxiety, or peace in my mind and body. It was that unscientific. I considered this the normal Christian life and was trying to do my best, like every other believer. But I had no track record or confidence in what was happening.

As a matter of fact, doubts besieged me after I told the Lord I would obey and call David.

"I'm still kind of new here. What if something goes wrong?" I asked while driving home from the office. "Is this crossing a line of professionalism? I don't even know what David Tyree believes or if he's a Christian. What if he's offended, or just thinks it's weird?"

Asking the financial advisor for permission to contact David was out of the question. For my boss, everything was about networking, leveraging relationships, making contacts, and expanding his business. "Make sure you get phone numbers," he would say as I went out the door to any meeting. He was the consummate networker, and I worried that he would think I was trying to ingratiate myself into David's life for personal gain.

"I could get fired for calling this guy," I thought. "There is no rational explanation for it."

Fear seized me.

"I can't do this. I really can't. It will upset the situation at work. It will ruin my reputation in the professional community. This could blow up so badly."

But I felt harassed by the Spirit. "Call him... Call David Tyree... Call David."

"And say what?" I wondered, but my question wasn't answered.

Finally, as much to restore my own peace of mind as anything, I committed to the Lord, "You win. I will call him Friday night after work. If something bad happens on that call, I'll have the weekend to figure out how to handle it."

The nagging feeling went away, replaced by a feeling of peace and resolve. I knew the Lord was expecting me to keep my word.

Thursday flew by and Friday dawned with renewed fears. All day I recoiled inwardly from the commitment I had made. The urge to call returned like an incoming tide, stronger with every wave, pounding my soul. "Call David…Call David Tyree."

I drove home feeling almost sick, ate dinner to steady myself, and at 8:30 p.m. pulled David's home number from my pocket. There was no backing down. I had to keep my commitment to the Lord. I nervously dialed, hoping the answering machine would pick up so I could hang up. The phone rang once.

Two rings.

Three rings. Fear rose with each passing second.

Four rings…no answer. I was ready to hang up. Then—

"Hello?" A man's voice. Live, not a recording.

My throat restricted as I forced out the words, "Is David there?"

"This is David."

"Hi, David. This is Hubie," I said.

A moment.

"Who?"

"Hubie. You know, the accountant."

"Oh yeah, man. How are you doing?"

"I'm fine," I said. I wasn't fine at all. I was shaking with fear. My career was on the line. But I soldiered on.

"Sorry to call you so late, but I have something that I have to talk to you about," I said.

"OK," he said, waiting.

"This isn't going to get any easier, is it?" I silently asked the Lord.

"Ever since I met you I have been praying for you," I said to David. "The Lord told me to call you because He wants to tell you a few things."

At this point the words began to flow beyond my control or comprehension. I could feel myself articulating them. They formed in my mouth one after another, almost like speaking in tongues. I knew the words were divinely energized, but I did not know what I was saying.

It seemed to go on for a while, and then it stopped.

Silence.

My thoughts jumped to warp speed. "I just made the worst mistake of my life. The guy probably thinks I'm crazy. How am I going to explain this to the advisor? I'm fired for sure."

Already wondering where I would look for other employment, I held on for David's response. There was none. Maybe he had hung up.

"David...are you there?" I asked.

"Yeah, I'm here. I just don't know what to say."

"Oh, God, I blew it," I thought. "What do I do now?"

He continued, "My wife and I were praying last night about some things, and we had a lot of questions. A lot of those things you just answered. You see, I play football, but what I really want is to share the gospel. I want a platform to share it with people, which is my desire. You said a lot of things, and one thing was that I would be known as a wide receiver, which is my dream. I am known as a special-teams player. I play the wide receiver position, but I am not known for that."

He paused a moment as if taking it all in.

"There was so much that you said that there was no way you could have known," he concluded.

Relief came upon me like a blanket. All the anxiety was suddenly gone.

"That's great, David," I said, feeling real peace for the first time in weeks. "I really don't know what I said, but I am happy for you and I will keep praying for you."

"I would like to get to know you better," David said. "Thank you for calling me, and for the word. We'll talk later."

"OK," I said, and we hung up.

A huge sigh of relief escaped me. I was so glad that was over. I slept soundly that night.

It occurred to me that David might mention our conversation to the advisor, but at work on Monday it was business as usual. David didn't say anything and neither did I. Everything had turned out OK.

THE CATCH

Soon after our call David invited my family over to meet his family. We spent time getting to know him, his lovely wife, Leilah, and their children. We shared a meal and prayer, talking about the Bible and how we all met the Lord. They couldn't get over how many kids we had. (Later the Tyrees would have seven.)

Vicki and I continued to pray for them in the following months. Soon Leilah was pregnant with twins. David's injury healed and he was back on the field with the Giants, but they weren't having a good season. They had lost the first two games and were 7–4 by Thanksgiving. David was playing special teams but caught just four passes all regular season as a receiver, none of them for touchdowns. To complicate things, David's mother died and he was grieving. I watched Giants games on TV to see David play and e-mailed or texted him now and then to offer encouragement. "I'm praying for you," I would say. "I know you're going to do well. God is with you." The urge to pray for him returned and was constant some days. "Lord, give him safety. Bless his family. Fulfill the word You gave to him."

The Giants were able to earn a wild card spot in the playoffs but were suffering from injuries to key players on offense and defense. We watched the team advance round after round, beating the Tampa Bay Buccaneers, Dallas Cowboys, and Green Bay Packers in those teams' home stadiums. My whole family became engrossed in the playoff run. We would pray for the Tyrees all week and watch David play on Sundays. To practically everyone's amazement, the Giants advanced to the Super Bowl to play the New England Patriots, who were undefeated and going for a perfect season—a feat accomplished just once before in NFL history.

I did not remember what God had said to David through me, and it was of no concern to me. I believed it was a private message and my part was done. But David had told others about it. A mutual friend mentioned that David was holding it tightly because it confirmed what he and his wife had heard from God. The word was, in essence, "God is going to bring you out of obscurity into the spotlight and give you a platform, and your name will go before you. You will be known as a wide receiver. I am about to highlight your skills as a wide receiver. I know about your desire to share your faith, and I am going to give you a platform to do that."

David mentioned to me later that I was the first one the Lord sent to the scene to help him through a rough season in his life. There were many others as well.

In the weeks before the Super Bowl Vicki and I prayed often for the Tyrees, and we began to feel a new quickening in our spirits: *something's going to happen.* Like a flickering flame in our hearts the sensation grew stronger as the game approached. We felt like kids on Christmas Eve, so excited because we knew something good was on its way. Neither of us had ever experienced such a feeling. When we prayed, the flicker in our spirits would dance even more. We felt certain that the Giants would win the Super Bowl and God would fulfill the word He had given to David by making him known as a wide receiver and giving him a platform to share the gospel. How it would happen remained a mystery.

The day before the Super Bowl the flickering was so intense that I couldn't sleep. I prayed for David throughout the night.

Family and friends gathered at our house to watch the game that Sunday in early February. The Giants were underdogs, and rightly so. The Patriots had gone 18–0 and were trying to become the first team since the 1972 Miami Dolphins to finish a season without a loss. In the first three quarters they showed why. The Giants were held to just a field goal in the first three quarters, stifled by the Patriots' defense. But the Patriots too had trouble scoring. When the fourth quarter arrived, the score was a skimpy 7–3 in favor of New England. The Giants looked tired and harassed, and David had caught just one pass. Still, we remained confident something would happen.

With eleven minutes left in the game, David lined up as a receiver and ran a route that put him open in the end zone. Giants quarterback Eli Manning zipped a pass to him, and David's catch gave the Giants the lead, 10–7.

We all celebrated, but I noticed something: the flickering in my heart didn't change. Catching the go-ahead touchdown was a good moment, but not *the* moment.

"I don't think that was it," I told Vicki, and she agreed. Something else was going to happen.

We found out later that on the day before the Super Bowl, David had the worst practice of his life. He dropped every single ball that was thrown to him. I could only imagine what that did to his confidence. Catching that fourth-quarter touchdown must have helped.

New England roared back, machine-like, to claim the lead with 2:42 left in the game, and things were looking dim. The Giants started their final drive on their own 17-yard line, and the Patriot defense looked primed to put the game away. Soon it was fourth down and a yard, and the Giants narrowly gained the first down with a two-yard run.

Two plays later Eli threw a pass in David's direction that was intended for another receiver who broke off his route. The ball sailed over David's head, and a Patriots defender got his hands on the ball. It looked like an interception would end the game. Instead, the ball bounced off both hands of the defender and sailed out of bounds incomplete. The defender stood there with his head in his hands, knowing that if he had made the play, the game would be over. With a minute and fifteen seconds left, the Giants were somehow still alive.

The next play was third down and five, and the Giants offensive line looked out of breath. As soon as the ball was snapped, the Patriots poured through. One lineman grabbed hold of Eli's shoulder, another the back of his jersey, and it appeared to be a sure sack. The pocket collapsed entirely, and for a moment Eli was almost invisible among the tumult of jerseys. Then, with a defender still grasping his jersey, Eli managed to slip into the open field and buy one more second. Far in the backfield he squared up and tossed the ball thirty-two yards into the middle of the field.

"It's to David! It's to David!" I said as the ball sailed through the air.

Sure enough, David was the intended receiver. He leaped high and grabbed the ball out of the air with both hands. Rodney Harrison, New England's star defender, hit the ball out of David's hands while he was in the air, and it looked as if it would fall incomplete. But instead of falling to the ground, the ball fell on David's helmet, and David's right hand pinned it there. Rodney tackled him, furiously trying to whack the ball loose, but David managed to put both hands on the ball and hold it against his helmet.

Vicki and I jumped up and screamed, "That was it! That was it!"

The flickering inside danced like a flame in the wind. We literally laughed for joy. I had never been so excited for a moment in sports. This was David's miracle, and it had happened before the eyes of millions.

Our friend Sinorice Moss, another receiver for the Giants, later shared his perspective of that play with us. Moss was watching from the sidelines when Eli threw the ball in the air. Moss stood up on the bench to see what would happen. When David made the catch, everyone on the sideline knew they would win the game, he said. Sure enough, a few plays later, Plaxico Burress caught the game-winning touchdown, and the Giants defeated one of the greatest teams in NFL history, the 18–1 Patriots.

We were so excited the rest of the night that we could hardly sleep. This time I wasn't interceding; I was rejoicing. "Look what God did," I kept thinking. "Thank You, Lord!"

I learned later that David's marketing guy was watching the game in a hotel room, and when David made the catch, this man fell to the floor and gave his life to Christ right there. He knew God had done it.

Early the next morning David called and left a message. He was weeping. "Hubie! Can you believe what happened? I can't believe it! Look what God did! I'm so speechless. I'm not going to take any credit for this. It's a platform, and I'm going to use it to share the gospel. I'll call you when I get back, and thank you for praying for me."

I couldn't have been happier. David had a platform to tell people about God, just as God promised. I knew he would use it well.

Nobody knew then that "the helmet catch" would go down in NFL history as the greatest catch in Super Bowl history and one of the greatest catches of all time. Sometimes spectacular plays like that are forgotten, but God elevated that moment. Today if you ask a football fan which teams played in the 2008 Super Bowl, few could give the right answer without looking it up. Who performed the halftime show? Who cares? Even the funny commercials are forgotten, as is the final score, the game MVP, and where it was all played.

But say "helmet catch," and most football fans break into a big smile. God made it one of the greatest and most unusual plays in Super Bowl history, a symbol of the ultimate clutch play by an underdog team. Nowadays when a receiver makes a great catch, you can hear the announcer say it is a "David Tyree–type catch."

David told us later that he didn't even know how

spectacular the catch was. He went up to catch the ball, and when Rodney hit it, David just reacted by holding it against his head. He didn't know how incredible it looked at the time.

Our friendship with the Tyrees would produce much more fruit than we expected. On a personal level, David gave me great counsel about how to raise a family and treat my wife, and how to handle challenging life situations. He even rebuked me on occasion. A lot of people have come and gone in David's life since that February day, but our friendship will always be special because of how God brought us together.

The experience also taught me several important things about how God works.

First, God will put us in places we don't want to be, to do what He wants us to do. What if I had quit working for the financial advisor before God did what He did with David? My own stubbornness might have caused me to miss the blessing of sharing the word with him.

Second, we can't let fear stop us from obeying God. What if I had been too afraid to call David and speak God's words to him? It would have been easy to think "practically" and say no to God's urging.

Third, as we follow God, we shouldn't expect Him to reveal the whole picture up front. Even after giving the word to David, none of us knew how or when it would be fulfilled. God has a way of stretching us by keeping us in the dark so we look to Him and not to our own abilities or knowledge. He will always be faithful to show us the way, one step at a time. Consider the examples set by Noah and Abraham:

> Now faith is the substance of things hoped for, the evidence of things not seen. . . . By faith Noah, being divinely warned about things not yet seen, moved with godly fear, prepared an ark to save his family, by which he condemned the world and became an heir of the righteousness that comes by faith. By faith Abraham obeyed when he was called to go out into a place which he would later receive as an inheritance. He went out not knowing where he was going.
>
> —Hebrews 11:1, 7–8

Faith means saying yes when we have no idea what it ultimately means. That's the kind of response that pleases God.

Fourth, when we step out to do the uncomfortable, God empowers us and gets all the glory. Our job is to show up, obey in spite of discomfort, and see how His Spirit moves through us. I love what Paul the Apostle wrote:

> For observe your calling, brothers. Among you, not many wise men according to the flesh, not many mighty men, and not many noble men were called. But God has chosen the foolish things of the world to confound the wise. God has chosen the weak things of the world to confound the things which are mighty. And God has chosen the base things of the world and things which are despised. Yes, and He chose things which did not exist to bring to nothing things that do, so that no flesh should boast in His presence. But because of Him you are in Christ Jesus, whom God made unto us wisdom, righteousness, sanctification, and redemption.

> Therefore, as it is written, "Let him who boasts, boast in the Lord."
>
> —1 Corinthians 1:26–31

> I can do all things because of Christ who strengthens me.
>
> —Philippians 4:13

> We have such trust through Christ toward God, not that we are sufficient in ourselves to take credit for anything of ourselves, but our sufficiency is from God.
>
> —2 Corinthians 3:4–5

> But He said to me, "My grace is sufficient for you, for My strength is made perfect in weakness." Therefore most gladly I will boast in my weaknesses, that the power of Christ may rest upon me.
>
> —2 Corinthians 12:9

Seeing how God moved in David Tyree's situation illuminated so many biblical principles and gave Vicki and me a foretaste of the life God had for us. We were two regular Christians with no real ambitions beyond local church ministry and occasional mission trips. I had no idea that God was preparing me to share divine messages with people from all walks of life—the famous, the unknown, and all those in between. I never would have chosen it for myself, and frankly it caused us a lot of discomfort and questions. But the results were obvious, as the words encouraged people far beyond what I could do in my natural abilities.

I'm still surprised because I'm just an accountant, a family man, a face in the crowd. For reasons I don't understand, God has given me work to do that goes beyond my wildest dreams. The good news is that I believe He has chosen you for a special work too. When you see the kind of dismal background I came from, you will know it's possible for you and that God has destined each one of us for extraordinary things, no matter where we came from.

Chapter 2

UNLIKELY PROPHET

It's an ugly story, but it's how my family began.

When my mother was fifteen years old, she was raped by a boy near a lake in Waco, Texas. My mother was a beautiful, black-haired, brown-eyed girl named Susie. Normally she picked cotton in the fields to help support the family. That day she, some relatives, and their friend took a welcome break to relax outdoors on a spring day. Susie had quit school after the fifth grade, and working in the fields was all she knew. There wasn't much time to play and be a kid. Now her childhood would come to an abrupt end.

As they walked along, her relatives decided to go exploring and left Susie with their friend. The two talked leisurely until her family members were out of sight. Then the boy jumped on her, stole her innocence, and fled before her relatives could respond to Susie's screams.

Feelings of shame and responsibility for what had happened engulfed Susie. Her father was furious and reported the crime to the police department, but the police did nothing about it. Susie was Mexican-American Indian, and in the sixties the police did not treat crimes against minorities with much seriousness. The horrible incident passed almost without public notice.

Susie realized she was pregnant with her rapist's child. Tormented by memories of the experience and by the burden she knew it would place on her family, she searched desperately for answers. One seemed to come in the form of a handsome Korean college student whom Susie's sister introduced her to. He was willing to take care of her and the baby, and she agreed to marry him even though he was twelve years older. The burden on her family was relieved, and marriage offered Susie an escape from the shame that single motherhood brought at the time.

The baby was born in February and named Matilda Synn. Susie became pregnant soon thereafter, and her second baby, this one by her Korean husband, was born the following March. She named him Hubert. Both children brought her great joy, but over time she began to cry a lot. She complained of being unhappy and eventually turned to smoking and drinking. My parents did not seem to love each other, and I felt little love from them, especially during my teen years. I concluded that I was the by-product of a "business deal." Nothing more.

As I grew older I realized that being a Korean Mexican American Indian kid in the South posed challenges. I looked different from everyone else. People made fun of me for my appearance and enjoyed pointing out how different my sister and I looked. She looked Caucasian, with white skin, brown hair, and brown eyes. She never had a problem making friends or feeling part of the crowd. I, on the other hand, looked Asian with my yellow skin, black hair, and brown eyes. Kids also made fun of my "grown up" name—Hubert. The teasing was so hurtful that I hated going to school.

One day I could take no more. A guy at school kept making fun of me, calling me Papa San and other ethnically insulting names. I saw a book sitting on my desk, and before I knew what I was doing, I grabbed it and slammed it against his face. Stunned silence gripped everyone around me. I was escorted into the hallway for a paddling from the teacher. "It was totally worth it," I thought.

From that point on, kids quit making fun of me and even seemed to fear me since I had defended myself so violently. I received a suspension, and that put me on the radar of the principal and other teachers who soon blamed me for things I didn't even do. That made me angry, and indeed the whole situation triggered a hot temper and anger streak in me that would take years to root out.

Captain of My Fate

I never felt I could put down deep roots because we moved around a lot. Whenever I found a group of friends, it seemed we were relocating again. My mother exhausted whatever answers she hoped to find in the bottle and returned to her spiritual roots by attending the Catholic Church and dragging us kids with her. Then, when we were living near St. Louis, she became born again at a full gospel evangelical church. Now I found myself in church services several times a week. I often heard people speaking in weird languages and saw them raising their hands. "What on earth is this?" I wondered.

One day during a service tears began pouring out of my eyes, and I did not understand why. I went to the altar and accepted Christ but did not know what it meant except that it stopped the flow of my tears. I started to attend church voluntarily but still didn't fit in with others, a theme that would carry into my adult life.

One day my dad came home from work and announced

that we were moving to New York City. I was terribly upset to leave the life I had built in suburban St. Louis. On the first day of school in New York City, I got beat up. "Welcome to New York," I thought. "Could it get any worse?"

It did get worse. I fell in with a crowd that was smoking, drinking, and doing awful things. Seeking acceptance, I merely created bitter memories for myself later. The only good thing to come from those years was meeting a girl named Vicki at a high school Asian club party. We offered each other a simple, "Hi, nice to meet you," and moved on. I had no idea this woman would later become my wife.

One day I came home to see my mother crying uncontrollably, her eyes swollen and red. She wouldn't tell me what was wrong but kept bursting into tears. This was new. That evening she sat me down.

"I've had enough," she said. "I'm going back to Texas. Your dad and I are getting a divorce."

She paused to give me time to absorb the terrible news.

"Hubert, do you want to go with me or stay here in New York?"

Shocked and numb, I thought for a moment and said, "I can't answer that now. I'm eighteen years old and not sure about my future."

That night I walked around the city thinking about my life. Nothing made sense. Things moved ahead in fits and starts punctuated by heartache, pain, and brief relationships. The only way to make my life better, I concluded, was to take control of it and stop relying on my parents and friends. I would set my own course. Nobody would hurt me anymore. I would trust myself and no one else. If I made a wrong choice, then I would deal with it, but I would never again rely on someone other than me.

My mother moved to Texas, and I stayed in New York

to graduate from high school and enroll in college. The adjustment was hard. Partying in high school carried few consequences, but in college it worked evil magic against my grades. I landed on the probation list and was in danger of being thrown out.

"Your GPA is 1.65, well below the standard," the guidance counselor informed me. "You need to raise it immediately."

I completely ignored the warning and kept partying. My grades the next semester flat-lined again. Now the guidance counselor's words were more direct.

"You're about to be thrown out of school."

"OK..." I thought. "I guess this is serious."

I couldn't shrug it off. Not-so-old fears of rejection returned with a vengeance. I couldn't suppress them anymore. On the subway home I thought about my future and the road I was on. Did I really want to continue this way? My life was about to go off a cliff, and I was the one driving the car. On that subway ride I bottomed out. If I had anything to live for, I couldn't think of it.

Remembering my commitment to steer my own ship and be the captain of my fate, I decided to try a new direction. If I could fail so well, maybe I could also succeed.

I got home and hit the books hard. Without quitting the part-time jobs I worked to pay for school, I used my remaining waking hours to yank up my grades. Never again did I struggle with school. Driven by fear and insecure pride, my life became very disciplined. By the time I graduated, I was on the dean's list and hungry for success in a career.

In my senior year I ran into Vicki again in a Vietnamese history class. We became friends and hung out. We studied and did homework together. As time went on, we started dating. Meanwhile I had several job offers and chose a small CPA firm in New York City. They were eager to give me as much responsibility as I could handle, and I started climbing the corporate ladder as fast as I could.

Vicki and I were married in 1990. From the start she was so gracious and kind, a shining example in my life. For my part, I was determined to create a life that was different from what my parents had created for me. I would not repeat their mistakes if I could help it.

A LIFE-CHANGING ACCIDENT

Our marriage seemed great, our careers were booming, and I thought we had found the key to living well. There's nothing like being young and successful in New York City to pump up your pride. Then one Sunday afternoon Vicki and I were grocery shopping. On the way out I bought beaded car seat covers because the fuzzy ones I had would get hot and sweaty in the warm weather. Little did I realize this purchase might have saved my life. I installed the seat covers before heading home, and off we went.

We had been having a good day, but now Vicki was acting strange—suddenly distant and quiet. "Did I say something to upset her?" I wondered.

"Are you OK, honey?" I asked her.

"I'm fine," she said, but the feeling in the car grew worse as the minutes passed.

"What's wrong?" I asked again.

"Nothing...nothing is wrong," she said unconvincingly. I glanced over and noticed she wasn't wearing her seat belt, which was strange. She always forced both of us to wear them even though I found it uncomfortable and restrictive.

Silence hung about us as we drove down city streets. Suddenly—*bang!* I felt myself thrust off the seat cover toward Vicki. Everything was in slow motion. I looked up and saw the windshield start to crack. Vicki screamed, and her passenger door window cracked. I grabbed her, pulled her down, covered her body with mine, and felt the glass from both windows shatter all over my back. The car skidded to a stop, and in those noiseless moments I stayed hunched over Vicki for what felt like a long time. Finally, I sat up to see what happened.

A car had run a stop sign and broadsided us. I managed to get out, but my legs felt numb. A guy asked if I was all right and said he had called 911. I walked around to try to get Vicki out through her door and saw that a large car had slammed into the passenger side of our small Mustang. I couldn't get Vicki out since my legs were injured, and now I was starting to feel pain. EMTs arrived and put us in the ambulance.

"It's a miracle we weren't hurt more," I thought during the ride to the hospital. The big car had pushed us into the opposite lane of traffic, but no one else had hit us. If Vicki had worn her seat belt, she would not have been flung out of harm's way. And the beaded seat cover had allowed me to slide to the middle and cover Vicki, shielding her from the flying glass.

What bothered me most was that this accident had happened though I had been driving safely. Nothing I did could have prevented it. That being true, I wondered, was I really in control of anything in my life? Or was I at the mercy of outside forces? Was my life even my own? Had I been lulled by a false sense of security? Before the accident I felt in command of life, running it as I planned. Now I knew I should have died or been badly hurt, through no fault of my own.

I also knew that something had protected us. I was determined to find out what it was.

Knee surgery followed, and driving proved a challenge. Thoughts about the accident ran nonstop in my head. But I would tell myself, "Lord, You spared us once, so if You are real, then we will be fine." I also used to recite Isaiah 54:17 over and over again: "No weapon formed against me shall prosper." Over time, by reminding myself of God's faithfulness, I overcame those fears. But while I believed God had spared our lives, the deeper questions abided. With a hunger I had never known, I began to seek Him. I prayed and searched the Bible for answers. The Holy Spirit led me to four scriptures I recalled from attending church as a teenager:

> Before I formed you in the womb I knew you; and before you were born I sanctified you, and I ordained you a prophet to the nations.
>
> —JEREMIAH 1:5

> Your eyes saw me unformed, yet in Your book all my days were written, before any of them came into being.
>
> —PSALM 139:16

> "For I know the plans I have for you," declares the LORD, "plans to prosper you and not to harm you, plans to give you hope and a future."
>
> —JEREMIAH 29:11, NIV

> And he gave some, apostles; and some, prophets; and some, evangelists; and some, pastors and teachers.
>
> —EPHESIANS 4:11–12, KJV

These four scriptures crystallized in my mind. They confirmed that the Lord had a plan for every person and gave each of us a special purpose and calling. They also indicated that He loves each of us, cares for us, and knows us individually before we are even conceived in our mothers' wombs. God willed each of us to be born; there are no mistakes.

Before this moment I had excluded myself from God's promises when reading the Scriptures because of my messed-up life. Unfairness and resentment had clouded my sight. Now I stood at a crossroads. Did the Lord really have a purpose for me? Was I that important to Him? Was His Word 100 percent true? Should I put my total trust in Him, or should I continue trying to live life on my own terms?

One day while I was praying and reading, the Holy Spirit powerfully opened up a passage to me:

> In the beginning God created the heavens and the earth. The earth was formless and void, darkness was over the surface of the deep, and the Spirit of God was moving over the surface of the water.
>
> God said, "Let there be light," and there was light. God saw that the light was good, and God separated the light from the darkness. God called the light Day, and the darkness He called Night. So the evening and the morning were the first day.
>
> —Genesis 1:1–5

The Lord told me, "I was hovering over the waters thinking what I was going to do, and then I started to create things. I did the same with you. Search My Word." The fact that God had thought about me and then created me was nothing short of stunning. As I searched the Bible, I saw it confirmed over and over again. The Lord had indeed thought about making me and had then done it for a purpose. *Amazing.*

I learned then that it does not matter how any of us started life. Like my sister, some are the product of rape. Like me, some are born into loveless relationships. Some births appear to be unintended, inconvenient, or even disastrous to the parents. None of that matters, because God willed each one of us to live. What matters is that we do what He created us to do during the life we have been given. The Lord knew each of us before we were born and put gifts and talents inside of us, even though it takes us time to discover what they are. He took the time to "think" about how to make you and everything that went into you. It insults your Creator to say He made a mistake by making you.

I saw in Scripture how the Lord chose ordinary, imperfect people to do great works for His kingdom. Mary the mother of Jesus was a simple, unmarried girl. David was a young shepherd boy and the least in his family. The most prominent disciples were fishermen. Abraham and Sarah were an elderly couple; so were Zechariah and Elizabeth, the parents of John the Baptist. There are no extraordinary people in God's plans. Indeed, He chooses the weak and foolish so that no one may boast about His work in their lives.

Our car accident didn't just wreck our car; it shattered my pride and self-conception. I had wandered so far from the truth that it took something big to overcome my blindness. Now I was ready to walk a new path and give God control of the life He had created. I marvel at how patient He was, how many times He forgave my complacency and selfishness. But I also marvel at how He encouraged and empowered me as I took each wobbly step toward the future He had preordained for me.

Where that future would take us, I had no idea. But I was ready to test the waters.

Chapter 3

PROPHETIC MINISTRY STARTS IN THE NURSERY

After the car accident and my subsequent surgery, Vicki and I began searching for a church. Both of us were card-carrying backsliders and had not taken faith seriously since our childhoods. Now we needed answers about the true meaning of life, who was in control, why we were on the planet, and what God had for us to do. At that point we had no clue about the kind of life God would lead us to, and we wouldn't have believed it if you told us. We were basically worldly people who could no longer make sense of things without appealing to something beyond ourselves. Our search for God was more desperate than noble.

Church shopping landed us at an old mainline church, and for a year we tried to plug in. It was probably better than nothing, and I was satisfied there, but Vicki, who had grown up with a more vibrant faith than I had, had become spiritually hungry and felt the teaching and relationships at the mainline church were too shallow. God continued to bring people into her path who had inexplicable joy, a glow—something different than what we had.

They were Christians who would say things like, "God told me this and that," leading Vicki to think, "I've never experienced that—but I want to." God was giving her a relentless desire for something more, which would soon change our lives.

Still, when Vicki suggested we attend a new church in Manhattan, I was a little wary.

Vicki's coworker, a Christian woman, attended a church with lots of show business people, and she invited us to their Easter concert. We lived in Queens, and the church was in Manhattan, so attending there every Sunday was already a nonstarter for me due to the commute. But Vicki had an unusual excitement about trying the place out. I was in the middle of tax season and decided to stay home, so Vicki journeyed there alone. When she returned, she told me that stepping into the church was unlike anything she had ever experienced; she physically felt the love of God wrapping around her. I saw a fire in her eyes that I had never seen before.

"This is what we have been missing," she told me. "You have to go there, honey."

The fact was that I wasn't looking for more in the same way she was. The accident showed me I needed God in my life, but I still felt He should fit neatly into my orderly plan. I was happy at the church we were attending. Maybe it wasn't exciting and full of glitzy people, but it didn't mess with my life either. Still, I couldn't ignore the effect this other church had on my wife, so I agreed that after tax season I would check it out. At the very least I was curious to find out what had impressed Vicki so strongly.

We attended a midweek service a few months later. We found ourselves among fifty or sixty other people who treated me very nicely though I was a stranger. As praise and worship time started, I noticed the singers could really sing and the musicians were awesome. I found out later that many were Broadway performers.

But it wasn't the musical talent that impressed me most. It was the sense of life, something fresh happening in the realm of the Spirit that I had never experienced before. My own spirit responded and witnessed inside of me, "This is where you should be." And so without fanfare we began attending regularly. I rededicated my life to the Lord, and that became our church home for the next several years.

As I reflect on that important decision, a couple of principles jump out at me. First, you have to go where God leads you. He has a specific place for you to be, certain people for you to be with, preplanned work for you to do, and an environment for you to grow in. The idea of church shopping is sort of backward. Instead of going out and choosing the place that matches your tastes, you should look for the place where God grabs you and says, "Here!" That's what He did with Vicki and me.

Second, God led us through Vicki. I had to submit to God's leadership through my wife, though I didn't see it that way at the time. I'm sure I thought I was leading us, once I decided the church was acceptable. In reality I was following the Holy Spirit's guidance. If for some reason I had proudly refused to go where my wife suggested we go, it would have divided our family, and I would have remained in a church where I wasn't growing as much spiritually. I shudder to think how important that decision was, and I didn't even know it at the time.

THE LOWEST ASSIGNMENT

God immediately began showing us how to be faithful in small and seemingly insignificant acts of service. My first ministry assignment was changing diapers and doing crafts with kids in the nursery.

Serving kids was not my idea. In fact, it was probably the last assignment I wanted, given my family history. But I was no good at what everybody else in the church was good at. I am completely tone-deaf, can't play an instrument well, can't sing, can't act, can't perform, and didn't seem to have any other noticeable gifts. I felt out of place and insignificant, and often wondered, "Where do I fit in at this church?"

One day someone asked if I could help in the children's ministry. Seeing no other open doors, I agreed and found myself among a bunch of nursery workers and little kids. All the other workers were women. "Oh, boy. This'll be fun," I thought, feeling more out of place than ever.

I stayed because I had given my word, and as the day progressed, it became clear I had certain skills most men don't have. One baby needed his diaper changed, and a female worker appeared too busy to do it. I volunteered, put the kid on the changing table, and changed his diaper in less than a minute. It presented no challenge at all because when I was growing up, my mother made me stay home against my will and help raise my younger brother and sister. As a result I knew how to burp and feed babies, change diapers, and warm bottles. I hated all of it and felt it was unfair that I had been pressed into service so early and missed out on playing with friends.

Now those skills served to impress.

"Look at that!" another worker said. "The man knows how to change a diaper correctly."

I smiled and said, "I've had a lot of practice."

As I said, it I could almost see the words in my head, "It was practice." I had never looked at changing my baby brother's and sister's diapers as practice; I considered it some sort of punishment. Now I saw that whatever we go through in life can be used by the Lord. Sometimes even the hard things are meant to shape our character or give us skills we need later on—even in the nursery.

Over the weeks and months ahead I learned more about myself than I thought possible. Shackled by feelings of rejection, bitterness, and injustice, I had become a selfish, controlling, and proud man. Serving others, especially children, was the last thing on my agenda. It brought up the same feelings I had when I was made to babysit my siblings or help my dad at his job. My heart had become bitter and angry, especially since my siblings were allowed to play while I worked. Childhood feelings of anger and resentment came out of hiding, and I had to grapple with them as I served in the nursery, a ministry assignment other people avoided. Spiritual growth and healing happened while I was missing "big" church to clean up kid messes and wipe spit off toys.

During those hours in the nursery God showed me that what I had "suffered" as a child could be used for His purposes. A light went on inside me, overpowering those dark feelings. Romans 8:28 now rang true:

> We know that all things work together for good to those who love God, to those who are called according to His purpose.

Great fulfillment came from knowing that parents could enjoy worshipping and hearing the Word preached because I and others were caring for their children. It gave meaning to the once-meaningless hours of labor I had put in as a boy. Soon I was serving in children's ministry three times a month with joy. I even noticed how kids seem to naturally obey men, and I was able to get some of the "out of control" kids in order, providing huge relief to the other workers. I also learned to teach the Bible in a very basic way, explaining the principles of God to little minds.

I thought I was volunteering to pay my dues. God used it to give me humility and healing I badly needed.

GO WITH THE FLOW

Time went on, and the church asked me to teach Sunday school and vacation Bible school to grade-schoolers. The differences in maturity jumped out at me. When I taught kindergarten-age kids, I almost always got through my lesson plan. The kids were open to whatever I had to say. Their main problem was talking when I was talking or not liking the snack. But in general they enjoyed the lessons.

Older kids seemed to come in with more problems and questions. Some would spit at each other, jab each other with pencils, or throw crayons across the room. Most thought they knew more about the Bible than I did. I soon learned how to handle that by making them an offer too good to refuse.

"If you can answer these questions about the Bible, then you can sleep the whole time," I said, and they eagerly agreed. "First question: How many of each animal did Noah bring on the ark?"

"Two of each," they said.

"Wrong," I said, and we read in Genesis that some animals were brought in twos, others in sevens.

"Next," I said. "What swallowed Jonah?"

"A whale!"

"Wrong again," and we read that it was a big fish that gulped down the prophet.

"Final question," I said. "What did Eve eat?"

"An apple."

I pointed out how the Bible didn't specify what kind of fruit was on the tree of the knowledge of good and evil. Deflated, they knew I had won fair and square and were more receptive to the lesson and to my leadership of the class.

It took me awhile to recognize that some interruptions were actually good. This happened especially when I started working with teenagers. As they get older, kids take longer to open up. Insecurity or unfair treatment at home or school send them scurrying inside of themselves. Some have lots of questions about the world around them. I watched certain kids go through stages of disruption and withdrawal before they finally opened up and began asking heartfelt questions.

At first I would get upset when peppered with these seemingly random questions during the lessons. I thought the kids were trying to derail the class. Then the Holy Spirit showed me that these were opportunities, indeed divine appointments that I should consider priceless. He wanted to help them with the issues of their hearts no matter what my particular lesson was that day. Success wasn't just about getting certain information into their heads; it was about following the Lord's leading moment by moment. That change of perspective would literally reshape how Vicki and I lived our daily lives, though it took many years.

I also began to appreciate God's wide range of diversity.

When you teach a lesson to kids from all kinds of racial and economic backgrounds, you quickly learn that everyone interprets life based on their own experiences. We literally think differently. I had to learn to appreciate the diversity God builds into everything, including His church. We must learn to respect and receive from people who are nothing like us. One time I took my family to a church that was in a ghetto. My kids had little in common with the kids there, and their minds had been shaped by totally different realities. That affected the way they learned the Bible, how they saw God, and much more.

This principle would be critical later when I began ministering to people prophetically. I knew from working with kids that people would interpret the same sentence very differently depending on their background. It forced me to be patient, to take time to listen to the person and make sure he understood whatever God was telling him.

As I recognized that the Lord was involved in each interaction with kids in Sunday school, I learned to be patient, show concern, and take time to listen closely to what the kids were saying. I didn't mind stopping the lesson to comfort them when they were upset or to speak to a personal concern. I learned to see that their efforts to disrupt often signaled a deeper hurt inside of them. God taught me to stop being so rigid and to go with the flow. Other teachers ran their classes like drill sergeants, a method I didn't think worked. Some were very lax, which also didn't work. I decided to aim somewhere in the middle. I wanted my kids to like me but also to respect and obey me as a teacher. The fact that I really cared about them seemed to command their attention. Asking "How was your week?" did a lot more than reading them the riot act.

Relatability

These days I interact with a lot of different people, some in deep and continuing relationships, others only one time for a few minutes. But God trained me in those children's Sunday school rooms to interact with everyone in such a way that it feels completely personal. And it is personal and heartfelt. I care for each individual I minister to now the same way I learned to care for each child in my class back then. I have noticed how some people with prophetic gifts go down the line impersonally. Because of the foundation God built in me during those years teaching Sunday school, I see prophetic ministry as a caring, relational experience.

If you think about it, God is relating to someone through you and giving him or her supernatural information to make the person feel loved, valued, and encouraged. If that isn't personal and loving, I don't know what is. For that reason people often tell me that the "words" I give them sound conversational, not didactic. What I enjoy most is sitting around the kitchen table having a good conversation with someone, and I feel the same way when I minister to people—it's just us at the kitchen table, talking about what the Lord has given us to know. That's also why I always ask people after I have ministered to them, "Do you have questions? Do you understand?"

Part of that is my natural temperament. I always figured I was good with kids because I had taken care of my own siblings. As I was teaching kids the Bible, I slowly realized that God has given me a natural ability to relate to people, to be approachable, to be a friend. Vicki had seen this from the start. When we were dating, she was often frustrated because friends would call and talk for hours, pouring out their problems to me. She called me Mr. Psychologist and was annoyed that my line was always busy (in the days before call waiting and cell phones). Of course, my relatability also attracted her because I enjoyed having conversations and was a good listener.

I didn't know it was a strength until I saw how my relationships with kids blossomed so easily. Some told me, "The best time of my week is coming to talk to you because you don't talk down to us. You care about how we feel." In Scripture I admired how Jesus ministered to the Samaritan woman at the well, who was culturally different from Him. His genuine concern drew her into a discussion about the good news. In the same way, Sunday after Sunday I was in a position where I had to relate to people of all kinds; all ages; all personalities, temperaments, and backgrounds. It honed my skill of finding a way to connect with people or figure them out with the help of the Holy Spirit.

Learning to minister to people one-on-one, as Jesus did, was one of the most important principles for using my spiritual gift and living the Christian life. Over time I saw it produce fruit in the lives of these kids, many of whom were from single-parent homes. They grew up and talked to me at church even when I was no longer teaching their class. One father even asked me to call his daughter to give her direction later in life. "She listens to you and doesn't listen to anybody else," he said, which was a sad thing to admit. But it showed me how powerful these principles are at building relationships between people and God.

Today when people express a desire to move ahead in their spiritual gifting, I urge them to allow the Lord to lay a foundation of humility, availability, and servanthood in their hearts. It may look like nursery work. It may look like something else. But unless we fall in love with unlovable tasks and hard-to-love people, He will never graduate us to higher things. I could easily have wallowed in bitterness about my nursery and Sunday school assignments, but God in His grace helped me to learn from them and eventually to treasure them. That is how God develops His heart in us, and the Bible says God notices:

> For the eyes of the LORD move about on all the earth to strengthen the heart that is completely toward Him.
>
> —2 CHRONICLES 16:9

> For we are His workmanship, created in Christ Jesus for good works, which God prepared beforehand, so that we should walk in them.
>
> —EPHESIANS 2:10

When people ask me how to get started in their spiritual gift, I say, "Find the lowest place and the lowest task the Lord will allow you to do, and do it with all your heart." That's how God began to transform my life and launch me into my spiritual gifts.

HEARING GOD IN HIS WORD

The other major change in my life was learning to make God's Word my basis for living. Long before God opened up my spiritual gifts to me, He taught me to hear Him in His Word, to love His Word, and to ground myself in His Word.

When I first started reading the Bible, I went straight to the red letters, Jesus's words. I wanted to hear what God Himself had to say. I also paid a lot of attention to Acts because it showed how God directed the believers' paths. Genesis fascinated me; I loved reading about Noah and the Flood, and how nobody listened to his warnings. That example and the Book of Acts showed me the powerful results that come from obedience to God.

Reading the Word showed me how endless and deep it is. The same verses would speak to me in different ways every time I read them. Changing translations helped me to get more out of the Bible as well. From the start I took obedience to the Word seriously. Hearing it was not enough. God speaks through His Word, and if we are not willing to obey, then we won't get good results.

The Bible says God's sheep hear His voice. "The sheep hear his voice, and he calls his own sheep by name and leads them out.... I am the good shepherd. I know my own and my own know me" (John 10:3, 14, ESV). Song of Songs 2:8 talks about "the voice of my beloved." Hearing God's voice in His Word drew me closer to Him and increased my hunger to find out how He ticks.

I didn't know it then, but learning to hear God's voice in the Bible was teaching me to hear His voice prophetically. God's prophetic words to us today always line up with His Word. The more familiar we are with God's character and ways, the greater our ability to discern His voice as He speaks today.

The Bible became my source for wisdom, comfort, stability, practical advice, and much more. If I was having a really bad day, I would read James. If I felt insecure, I would read Jeremiah and see how God had chosen him, "molding and shaping" him for a predestined purpose. If I wanted to explore prophetic stuff, I would read Isaiah. Psalms spoke to me many times when I was upset or struggling to fit in with other people. God would show me how David didn't fit in with people.

Whenever I needed comfort, I would open the Bible and find something that pertained to me. This wasn't

Bible roulette; it was searching the Word for answers. Sometimes it took awhile. I knew answers were in there; I just had to look for them. I never failed to find an answer to my specific situation when I turned to the Word. I also listened to lots of sermon tapes and Christian radio shows. I was a faithful listener to *Focus on the Family*, *Leading the Way* with Michael Youssef, and a little-known regional pastor named Jonathan Cahn whose radio show was called *Two Nice Jewish Boys*. Hillsong and other Christian music filled my family's cars and our home.

Mission trips were particularly valuable in making the Word come alive. When you see God answer prayer and lead you supernaturally in ministry on the mission field, you feel almost like part of the Book of Acts. It connects those stories to today. It also helped that the people I traveled with played Bible trivia games, and they knew a lot of stuff. I picked up a bunch of knowledge just by hanging out with Bible fanatics.

The more I obeyed the written Word of God, the more I desired to read it and learn about God's character and ways. The more I grew to know and love God, the more I developed "ears to hear," and the easier it became to discern His voice. A submitted heart allows the Holy Spirit to move freely in you. Cultivating a relationship with God and obeying His Word are some of the most important first steps to hearing what God has to say today.

Discovering the Supernatural

At our new church Vicki and I also were exposed to the supernatural working of God like never before. Vicki had grown up in a conservative Baptist church and was saved as a child, but she was taught that the only interaction you could have with God was praying and sensing peace about a decision, or noticing a certain principle in the Bible. The idea of God speaking to people today was alien to both of us. He seemed distant and uninvolved.

On mission trips I was now seeing stuff I could hardly imagine. In Africa during a particular church service we were leading, one woman began yelling and screaming, her eyes bouncing around weirdly and her arms making snaky dancing motions. The hair on my neck stood straight up.

"You must stop," the pastor declared from the pulpit.

"I will not stop!" the woman yelled back.

Then the pastor did the most unexpected thing. The minister turned to me and said, "You go get her."

"What?" I said.

Bravely another guy and I got up and apprehended the woman. She was surprisingly strong and resisted us as we grabbed hold of her. The pastor came down and prayed for her, at which point she fell on the floor and squirmed around like a snake. I had never seen someone demon possessed, and it freaked me out. But when the pastor rebuked the demon and caused it to leave, the woman looked completely different and totally normal. "Whoa! This stuff is real!" I thought.

Another mission trip to Ethiopia was almost canceled because our ministry opportunity fell through. But we felt God wanted us to go anyway and would open other doors. We boarded the plane for the long flight, arrived in Addis Ababa, and proceeded to sit around the hotel for two days waiting on God. Two women from our team were having lunch, and a waiter noticed them praying. He invited them to meet with his pastor, and before we knew it, our team was ministering to a gathering of ten thousand people.

Only God could do that.

Back on home soil our church held a concert in the park. It was raining and the sky was thick with clouds. We went backstage to pray for the rain to stop, and as we went on stage, the clouds parted and the sun came through. The sunshine lasted just as long as the concert, and as soon as we finished, the rain began pouring again.

God moved in our personal lives too. For example, Vicki left her job at a large consumer products company several times, but every time she returned to work for them, she would get a promotion. It made no sense, but God was showing us He could advance us no matter the circumstances.

My whole family began to see the supernatural as normal. One day my daughter Sara came home and said, "I don't need my glasses anymore, Daddy."

"What are you talking about?" I asked. She had worn glasses from a young age.

"I prayed and God healed my eyes," she said. "I don't need glasses anymore."

She was very matter-of-fact about it. I could only think, "I want that." I had worn glasses for years.

Upstate New York was my destination a few weeks later, and I was driving up to what promised to be an unpleasant business meeting. I was the accountant for a ministry where a theft occurred, and I was being blamed for not preventing it. It was an ugly situation, and I was innocent of what I was being accused of. I spent most of the two-and-a-half-hour drive fuming about it to the Lord.

"I can't believe You're making me do this," I complained. "I volunteer for a minimal fee to help this ministry, and look what they do to me."

Suddenly I felt something like sand in my left eye. Now I was even angrier. "I'm going to give these people a piece of my mind," I promised. I rubbed the eye but only irritated it more. Now it was getting hard to drive.

Then my right eye started to tear up as well. I could barely see.

"Great, Lord! Now I'll probably be in an accident," I complained.

"Be quiet," the Lord responded, "and take off your glasses."

I was nearsighted, so I could not see far distances. But when I took off my glasses, I could see far again with clarity as I had been able to in my teenage years. Tears poured from my eyes. "I'm sorry," I said more than a few times. I was so dumbfounded I could hardly process what had happened.

"You look different," the CEO said when I arrived. "What's going on with you?"

"God healed my eyes. I can see!" I said, showing him the now-useless pair of glasses I held in my hand.

"Praise God!" he said, smiling.

The meeting went as well as expected, and the drive back was full of praise—as the drive up should have been.

ALASKAN LESSONS

Some of my most intense growth took place on my first mission trip to Alaska. I had been serving in the children's ministry for about a year and felt the Lord leading me to join the Alaska trip, but I considered myself an unlikely missionary. I didn't have time, money, or desire—but none of that mattered to God. He had potent lessons about humility, servanthood, and the power of praying in the Spirit in store for me there.

My roommate was a guy named Jack Forde who had

been a Christian a lot longer than I had. We talked for a while one night, and I fell asleep around midnight. A few hours later I woke up to the sound of Jack talking. I peeked and saw him pacing the floor, praying. "This guy's really into it," I thought. I pretended to be asleep and listened to him pray for everyone on the trip by name. This went on most of the night.

My eyelids were heavy the next morning. The team met and shared what the Lord was revealing to us in our private prayer times. I could hardly believe when the other team members brought up many of the issues Jack had been praying about the night before. "What a coincidence," I thought.

That night Jack and I talked again about our experiences and the Bible. It was fascinating how excited he was about Scripture. At 2:00 a.m. I heard Jack get up and start pacing the floor praying for everyone again, even the people that bothered him. "That's amazing," I thought. My feet hit the floor and I joined him, praying for everyone by name until the sun rose. Before we knew it, the sun was rising. At the morning devotional meeting, every topic of discussion was again exactly what Jack and I had discussed and prayed about the night before. "This is unbelievable," I thought. "Two days in a row!"

Up to that point the only times I prayed were at church, before meals, and before bed. Seeing Jack pray and seeing God reveal what would happen the next day ignited my desire for more. Even Jack's laugh had real joy in it. I decided to keep praying through the night with Jack the rest of the trip.

For ten days God revealed things to us in late nights of prayer that other people later shared as prayer concerns or words from God at morning devotions. It blew my mind. Jack also woke me up a few times to give me an encouraging or directive word, and the words were amazingly accurate. Just as remarkable to me was how much peace I felt when I kept praying, even in hectic times. I was learning to pray without ceasing.

I noticed that the more I prayed, the more sensitive I became to how the Holy Spirit communicated with me. When we shared the gospel with people on the streets, I could discern whom to talk with and whom to avoid. Peace came over me when I saw someone God wanted me to speak to. An uncomfortable feeling met me when I saw someone God did not want me to approach. This pattern proved consistent, and this sense was not emotional. I did not feel "happy" or "sad." Rather I had a "knowing" that I learned to discern. Hebrews 5:14 tells us discernment comes through having one's senses exercised, which means it takes practice:

> But strong meat belongeth to them that are of full age, even those who by reason of use have their senses exercised to discern both good and evil.
>
> —KJV

The Word of God also says:

> I will instruct you and teach you in the way you should go; I will counsel you with my eye on you.
>
> —PSALM 32:8

> Your ears shall hear a word behind you, saying, "This is the way, walk in it," whenever you turn to the right hand and when you turn to the left.
>
> —ISAIAH 30:21

I paid close attention to what I was sensing so I could learn the ways of God. I soon noticed that through times of extended prayer I was more aware of His presence. I saw a different side of God—the close and personal God who walks with us through life. I prayed and asked Him to show me how to pray in the Spirit at all times, day and night, even when at work or doing other things. He did just that, showing me how to go through the day knowing He is right next to me and available for ongoing conversations. Prayer is not just about approaching God formally but interacting with Him throughout the day as I would with a person. Ephesians 6:18 says, "Pray in the Spirit always with all kinds of prayer and supplication. To that end be alert with all perseverance and supplication for all the saints."

This way of walking and talking with God changed my life completely. It was possible to hear Him clearly and allow Him to direct my steps throughout the day. If I stayed close in prayer, then I wouldn't have to do anything special to get in tune with God, because I was in tune with Him all the time. The Word says as much:

> Have not I commanded you? Be strong and courageous. Do not be afraid or dismayed, for the LORD your God is with you wherever you go.
>
> —JOSHUA 1:9

> And remember, I am with you always, even to the end of the age.
>
> —MATTHEW 28:20

> Fear not, for I am with you; be not dismayed, for I am your God. I will strengthen you, yes, I will help you, I will uphold you with My righteous right hand.
>
> —ISAIAH 41:10, NKJV

> Do you not know that you are the temple of God, and that the Spirit of God dwells in you?
>
> —1 Corinthians 3:16

I also learned in Alaska that no job was too humble for me. My purpose on the trip was to float around and help anyone who needed it. That included running errands to local stores and doing grunt work no one else wanted to do. It was a tough pill to swallow. Back at work I was the boss, the head honcho, while the administrative assistants did the "menial" jobs. That mentality colored my approach to ministry. "Shouldn't I be doing the kind of work I'm qualified for?" I wondered as I fetched things for people.

It was an important kingdom lesson: humility is the gateway to all ministry. Ugly pride and desire for recognition permeated my heart. God brought this to the surface where I could see it, and boy, was it unpleasant. Now I was stuck in a situation where I had to humble myself to be helpful. It was uncomfortable but necessary. Philippians 2:1–5 tells us:

> If there is any encouragement in Christ, if any comfort of love, if any fellowship of the Spirit, if any compassion and mercy, then fulfill my joy and be like-minded, having the same love, being in unity with one mind. Let nothing be done out of strife or conceit, but in humility let each esteem the other better than himself. Let each of you look not only to your own interests, but also to the interests of others. Let this mind be in you all, which was also in Christ Jesus.

Ephesians 4:1–3 encourages us to "walk in a manner worthy of the calling with which you were called. With all humility, meekness, and patience, bearing with one another in love, be eager to keep the unity of the Spirit in the bond of peace." First Peter 4:10–11 teaches us, "As everyone has received a gift, even so serve one another with it, as good stewards of the manifold grace of God. If anyone speaks, let him speak as the oracles of God. If anyone serves, let him serve with the strength that God supplies, so that God in all things may be glorified through Jesus Christ, to whom be praise and dominion forever and ever."

Those ten days in Alaska taught me that humility and prayer are foundational characteristics of any ministry. God was so faithful to send Jack to open my eyes to the power of prayer so I would be sensitive to receiving the revelation of God's purposes for each day. Ministry, I realized, was not about my agenda or skills. God had a plan and a path; my responsibility was to walk in it.

Maybe you are asking, "Where do I start? How do I grow in my natural abilities and my spiritual gifts?" Let me assure you, God has a plan and will reveal it as you make yourself available to serve. Your God-given, God-designed destiny involves a journey of learning, training, and pruning before you reach the fullness of your calling. Our heavenly Father is looking for those who are willing to say yes to the call even when the beginnings look small and humble.

Oh—and He's going to demand your wallet too.

Chapter 4

LETTING GO OF THE BANK ACCOUNT

WHAT DO FINANCES have to do with growing in your spiritual gift? A lot more than you might think.

God does not need your money, but money is a crucial way He teaches us to surrender ourselves and steward His resources. Surrender and stewardship of money teach us to faithfully manage our spiritual gifts as well. I believe finances are one of the most important training grounds to get us ready for greater things in the Spirit. In fact, to hear from God in an ongoing, accurate way, I believe you must fully surrender your finances and get rid of the ownership mentality. We are managers of what God gives us, and He gives it for His purposes, not ours.

This was a tough lesson for me because my mother didn't handle money well, generally speaking, and I felt my siblings and I suffered for it. My father worked and gave my mother a certain amount of grocery money to take care of household needs. My mother grew up poor and didn't even attend junior high school, so she didn't know how to spend money wisely. Her method of shopping was to find whatever canned food was on sale and pour the contents over white rice for dinner. Nobody ever taught her to cook, so there were some pretty strange combinations.

The best lesson my mother taught me was to give cheerfully, but I didn't accept the lesson until later because it meant such hardship for my siblings and me. After she met the Lord, she happily gave away anything she could. She treated the grocery money as "income" and paid "tithe" on it to the Lord. She then gave an offering besides that, and soon the money was down to two-thirds of what my father had given her. Every televangelist who promised something in exchange for a "love gift" received an envelope of cash from my mother. Our house was littered with prayer shawls, prayer cloths, gospel music cassettes and albums, Bibles and more Bibles, yet we kids sometimes went hungry because the fridge was empty. We didn't even know these evangelists, and my mother was putting them ahead of us. I pictured them living comfortably while we scraped by. Resentment built up inside me.

A few times my mother gave away almost all the money, and we were left with nothing to eat. I remember my sister and I eating an old fruit cake that had been sitting around the house for a while, hoping it was still good. On another occasion a jar of mayonnaise became a meal. From the first spoonful I felt sick. To this day I rarely eat mayonnaise. Kids at school always seemed to have plenty of good food, but my mother's generosity left us lacking.

My mother always insisted that God would give us everything we needed. I didn't buy it. One day we were walking to the local Laundromat, and my mother said, "The Lord told me this morning that He was going to give me $100."

"Yeah, sure," I thought to myself. "All you do is give those Jesus people our money."

We crossed the street and stepped over a puddle near the curb. My mother glanced down, and the next thing I knew, she had pulled a very soggy $100 bill from the puddle. "Praise God," she said. "See? He doesn't let me down." I was dumbfounded but refused to give God credit because I was too bitter over our family's apparent poverty. Why would I want to follow in my mother's footsteps? I made up my mind to hold tightly to my money when I grew up. When I graduated college and started earning my own income, my main financial goals were to buy whatever I wanted and not be taken advantage of by others. I had no concept of giving God control over my finances. Even as a newly recommitted believer I wasn't ready to trust Him.

Financial Failure

This mind-set was challenged when we joined the Manhattan church and heard about God and His principles of financial stewardship. I had a hard time accepting the idea of giving money and possessions away. And as a certified public accountant I was trained to check numbers and value every cent. That played into my distrust and suspicion over how the church was using its funds. Memories of going hungry haunted me. I didn't want my family to be taken advantage of by another ministry.

Over time I read a number of stories in the Bible about people giving generously and receiving back from God. A widow used the last of her food to make a meal for Elijah (1 Kings 17:7–16). Early Christians shared their possessions with those in need (Acts 4:32–35). Barnabas gave land away and increased in authority in the early church (Acts 4:37). Jesus said that whatever measure we use will be given back to us, pressed down, shaken together, and running over (Luke 6:38).

"Fine for them," I thought. "They didn't live in modern New York City."

We also were taught that God has the power to supply and restore finances and material goods as He wills. The Word states plainly:

> All the earth is Mine.
>
> —EXODUS 19:5

> Behold, to the LORD your God belong heaven and the highest heavens, the earth and all that is in it.
>
> —DEUTERONOMY 10:14, NAS

> Everything under heaven is Mine.
>
> —JOB 41:11

> The earth is the LORD's, and everything in it, the world, and all who live in it.
>
> —PSALM 24:1, NIV

These scriptures were pretty black-and-white, but I stubbornly held on to my opinion—and my money. I thought Bible people set a good example, but that was a long time ago. Reality had changed. My job was to behave wisely with my money, which meant not giving it away cavalierly as my mother had. I didn't yet understand the lesson my mother had tried to teach me, that when you don't have a giving mentality, you develop an entitlement mentality and eventually your wealth comes to nothing. That's exactly what happened to us.

Vicki and I had full-time jobs and treated ourselves to whatever we wanted, using credit cards at will. We felt we deserved material possessions to make up for what we lacked growing up. Foolishly we justified our spending by looking only at the credit cards' fifty dollar minimum monthly payment due instead of the balance we were carrying. I'm not sure how I passed that by my CPA brain, but I did. We were young and selfish.

Debt crept up and pounced on us. Soon we were working to pay all the credit card bills, with little left over. Living beyond our means had trapped us. My financial management had driven us into a ditch.

One Sunday I spoke to a couple at church named John and Annie Cavazos. The conversation turned to finances, and John asked me point-blank, "Do you tithe?"

"Er...um...no," I replied, feeling rightly embarrassed.

He stared at me and said, "You know, that is really the problem."

"This guy thinks not tithing is my problem," I thought, dismissing it. "I'm an accountant, and I know my issues are overspending, student loans, and other obligations." I was looking at our bank account on a natural level, while John was looking at it on a spiritual level. He was right, but it took us awhile to figure that out.

Soon after this conversation our financial situation worsened. We had maxed out our credit cards, and the creditors raised our interest rates and minimum payments. With no other earthly answer, we decided to try tithing.

We lacked faith to give the full tenth of our income, which is what a tithe is, so we gave what we were comfortable with. As the weeks went by, we felt convicted by the Holy Spirit to give a full tithe. Other church members had given testimonies of supernatural deliverance from debt and cited tithing as the reason. Encouraged by their testimonies, we decided to trust God with our financial situation and give the full 10 percent. It meant our bills would be paid late, which made no sense to us, but we did it out of desperation as much as obedience. We had no guarantee that the Lord would deliver us from debt, but we consciously decided to believe that He would.

The Holy Spirit didn't stop there. He then compelled us to give offerings to missionary funds, vacation Bible school, and to people in need—all on top of our tithe. On a fleshly level I could hardly sleep because our bills were late and, just as my mother had done, we were giving our money away to ministries. But in my spirit I felt peace and joy because I knew I was being obedient with my finances. I also saw these ministries benefit directly from our giving. Only that and the sense of peace convinced me that we were not being irresponsible.

Financial relief didn't come immediately, but during that season of struggle God taught me how to hear from Him when it came to giving. A pattern emerged: Sometimes I would feel an urge to give and would have a sense of excitement about the ministry purpose. Having given, I felt a sense of deep peace and joy, and knew that everything would be OK. Other times I did not feel moved to give an offering toward a need. Instead, I felt uninterested and just wanted to sit still and not participate. I knew this wasn't just my capricious emotions but the promptings of the Holy Spirit. I'm sure He did it to teach me what His leading was like.

Two years after we started tithing, our lawyer called. We had retained him after the car accident to help us recoup lost wages and medical bills from our injuries. He had said it would take years for the case to be settled. Now he informed us that out of the blue the guy who hit us was taking all the blame and wanted his lawyer to settle the case quickly. I asked how much they were offering to settle for, and to my amazement the settlement amount, after our lawyer's fee, was the exact amount we needed to get out of debt. God supernaturally erased our debt in one afternoon and even turned a circumstance the enemy meant for harm into good. (See Romans 8:28.) Needless to say, we have tithed and given offerings faithfully ever since.

In fact, we began giving as much as the Lord would allow us to. Vicki in particular discovered the joy of giving to people in need or just because God wanted to bless someone. What a blessing it was to stop being concerned about money because God was faithful to replenish and supply our needs as we were obedient. The expressions on people's faces when they received a gift was priceless. "Really?" they would say. "The Lord told you to do this for me?" The joy and satisfaction was as real for us as for them.

One time I went too far without Vicki's approval. I was praying and the Lord told me to bless a family by giving them one of our cars. We owned two cars, and Vicki didn't drive hers much—so I chose to give hers away. When I saw the husband next, I threw him the keys to Vicki's car. "The Lord told me to give it to you. It's yours," I said. Shock swept over his face. He was blessed, big-time, and I felt such joy from the Lord.

As I walked back to our apartment, it dawned on me that I had given away Vicki's car without discussing it with her. "No wonder it felt so easy," I thought. "I might be in big trouble."

Vicki got home, and I tried to think of a way to tell her I had just given away her car. When the truth finally came out, she was really upset. I pleaded with the Lord to get me out of trouble, and He provided a brand-new truck for Vicki in a matter of days. Still, it was a lesson learned: always do things in unity.

GOOD-BYE, STRATOCASTER

We were getting good at giving stuff away. Then God targeted my most prized material possession.

I had bought a beautiful white Fender Stratocaster at a music store in Manhattan. It was the perfect guitar for me and seemed to make my playing sound better, something even the people in church noticed. I didn't know how to play well, but I tried my best to blend in. I would strum lightly or turn down the volume on the guitar so no one could really hear me. I was always scared to make a mistake since the people I was playing with were real musicians.

While packing my bags for a missionary trip to Sweden, I lovingly put the guitar in its case and gazed at it for a moment. I could not wait to play it with the music ministry team overseas. At that moment the Holy Spirit distinctly spoke to me: "You are going to give it away to someone in Sweden."

"That can't be true," I thought. "I love this guitar so much. It seems to be made especially for me, and I was fortunate to have found it."

All guitar players have a guitar they feel is the "one." It takes on their personality and expresses them best when they play. That was my Stratocaster. I had bonded with the instrument like a lifelong friend.

The Holy Spirit, of course, did not care about that.

We arrived in Sweden and began to minister in music. I knew by then that my guitar was indeed going to someone else, so I began trying to argue my way out of it.

"Is this really happening?" I asked the Lord. "What am I going to do after I give it away? I won't have a guitar to play on this trip. How will I explain it to the music ministry team?"

We ministered for eleven days, and God was quiet about the guitar. I started to think I had dodged a bullet. "Oh well, guess I'll just have to keep it," I thought with deep satisfaction.

The day before we left for home, we rehearsed at a church for our last night of ministry. From my position onstage I saw a young kid sitting in the front row looking at me. I smiled. Then the Holy Spirit whispered to me, "That one!"

I ignored His voice and kept playing the song.

"That one!" the Spirit said joyfully. "That one!"

The words filled my ears, and finally I replied, "That one, what?"

"That young man is the one who is going to get your guitar."

"I was so close to keeping it," I thought.

Rehearsal ended. We walked back to the hotel, and I asked if anyone knew the kid who was in the front row. Someone said he was a pastor's son named Jonatan. Back in my room I opened the Stratocaster case and looked at the beautiful instrument. I sighed.

"You're going to have a new owner," I said. "We have one more time to play together, and then it's good-bye."

My friend Jack came in, looked at me, and asked what was wrong. When I told him what I had to do, he smiled. "God has a purpose," he said, and with those words I felt peace and a willingness to part with the beloved instrument. I wouldn't say I was overly happy, but there was a certain joy in knowing I was doing what the Lord wanted me to do. I knew my heavenly Father would be proud of me.

The ministry that night was great. Scanning the audience, I spotted Jonatan, and after the service I motioned him over.

"Would you mind holding my guitar while I pack my

gear?" I asked. He gladly agreed, and I saw him gaze at it as I usually did.

"How do you like it?" I asked.

"It is great! It is so beautiful," he said. "In Sweden, a guitar like this is very expensive because it is made in the United States."

I knew nothing about this kid, not even if he played the guitar. We talked for a bit about music and ministry, and then I said, "The Lord has a calling for you. Do you know that?" He nodded. I continued, "The Lord knows everything about you, and to prove it, the guitar you are holding is now yours." He was speechless, and I believe he nearly fell out of his chair. "God has a calling for your life, and you are responsible now since you have been equipped," I said.

"I don't understand and I don't know what to say. Why are you doing this?" he asked.

"You don't need to say anything. Just do what the Lord is telling you to do." I grabbed my backpack and decided to head out before the moment could get to me. "Be cool," I said as I walked away from Jonatan and the Stratocaster.

On the way back to the hotel, people looked at me quizzically. "Where's your guitar?" they asked. "Did you forget it? Was it stolen?" It hurt so much that I just kept walking and didn't even make eye contact.

"My guitar has a new owner," was all I said.

"Just keep walking," said Jack, who was beside me. His words encouraged me.

The next morning while I packed to leave, the Lord gave me Jude 20–22: "But ye, beloved, building up yourselves on your most high faith, praying in the Holy Ghost, keep yourselves in the love of God, looking for the mercy of our Lord Jesus Christ unto eternal life. *And of some having compassion, making a difference*" (KJV, emphasis added). I knew that was what I had done for Jonatan.

Home was a little quieter those next few months, and I tried not to dwell on the loss too much. One day our pastor received a letter from a pastor in Sweden, Jonatan's father. The man wanted to thank whoever had given his son the guitar. Jonatan had been struggling to play guitar for the church, he said, because the church's guitars were of such poor quality, and he was having a hard time learning on his own. He had told God one night that he was going to quit playing guitar unless God clearly showed him to keep going. That was the night I gave Jonatan my guitar. Jonatan became the head of a youth ministry in Sweden and used the guitar story as part of his testimony.

If you are wondering how I was so sure I was hearing from God in that situation, the answer is, I wasn't. I was learning to recognize His voice and the signs He gave me along the way. It took practice. Sometimes I got it right, and sometimes I got it wrong. I learned that sometimes His voice is still and small in my head. Other times it takes the form of an "urging." Still other times His leading is obvious when circumstances and details line up and make sense. And other times the direction seems to come out of left field.

The best thing in all situations is to obey out of a pure motivation. One of the greatest lessons I learned is to trust God to cover me and correct my course if I make a mistake while trying to be obedient. Think of it this way: If God showed you grace by cleaning up the mistakes you made as a new Christian and before you came to Christ, how much more grace will He cover you with now that you are walking with Him and trying to be obedient? Romans 5:10 tells us, "For if while we were enemies, we were reconciled to God by the death of His Son, how much more, being reconciled, shall we be saved by His life."

But in the case of my Fender Stratocaster, I had heard God right. Through my obedience a future leader in the Swedish church was blessed and emboldened in his work for the Lord.

GIVING GOD OUR JOBS

The next level of obedience and trust was bigger than Vicki and I ever expected: Were we willing to give God control of our employment? It's one thing to give a gift here and there, even a nice guitar or your automobile. It's quite another to give up your very source of income.

God's financial favor had been upon me since I started practicing accounting. I grew quickly in responsibility within the firms for which I worked. In addition to my full-time job, individuals and small business owners often approached me to be their accountant and then referred my name to their friends. I never solicited business or gave out business cards. God just sent clients, clients, and more clients. My side business soon became too inconvenient to practice out of the home. I wasn't absolutely sure, but it seemed the Lord was leading me to quit my full-time job to build my own accounting practice. To do that would require an office in Manhattan where most of my clients were located. Rental space was $18,000 a year, more than the $14,000 a year my accounting business was making at the time. Yet I felt God persistently urging me to sign the lease. With a deep breath I quit my job and signed the lease on my own office space. I'm pretty sure the signature was shaky because I was so scared.

God was faithful, and business multiplied right after I

moved into the office. My income was not yet high enough to replace the salary I had left, but Vicki was working full-time so we felt secure in her steady paycheck and health insurance coverage.

Then the Holy Spirit led Vicki to resign from her job to take care of our growing family. We almost couldn't believe He was doing this. "Could this really be of God?" we asked. "How could He ask us to give up her salary too? What will we do about health insurance? We have a toddler and another baby on the way. Why would God ask us to do this?"

Once we accepted that the leading was from God, we wondered about the timing. It made sense that Vicki should wait to quit until my business was big enough to cover both our salaries, but of course the Holy Spirit had His own timeline. He began waking Vicki up in the middle of the night, every night, to tell her, "Now is the time." This went on for weeks. The voice in her head was so clear and distinct that it seemed God was in the bedroom speaking to her in person, she said.

In fear, trembling, and perplexity Vicki gathered the courage to resign from her job. We were beside ourselves with worry when she came home that night. I took out the small shaving can "safe" where we stored our money. We sat on the futon, and I unscrewed the bottom of the can and pulled out $900. That was our savings, all we had. I hugged Vicki, and we both started crying out of fear. Then we turned our tears toward God and cried out for help, hoping we hadn't made a huge mistake. To our astonishment, my accounting practice grew even more quickly after that. God sent me new clients left and right. All our needs were met. I didn't network or advertise, and still God sent new clients or additional work whenever needs arose. I also expanded into business advising, helping clients grow their businesses. In a few years I had a full-time staff member and up to three part-time employees during busy seasons.

God used each step of faith to teach us about stewardship and to break our entitlement mentality. We stopped loving our money and possessions and gave up control of our finances. No matter how uncomfortable we felt at times, God always came through for us. We trusted Him to take care of all our needs, no matter how big or small. Matthew 6:25–34 came to mind many times:

> Therefore I say to you, do not worry about your life, what you will eat or what you will drink; nor about your body, what you will put on. Is not life more than food and the body more than clothing? Look at the birds of the air, for they neither sow nor reap nor gather into barns; yet your heavenly Father feeds them. Are you not of more value than they? Which of you by worrying can add one cubit to his stature?
>
> So why do you worry about clothing? Consider the lilies of the field, how they grow: they neither toil nor spin; and yet I say to you that even Solomon in all his glory was not arrayed like one of these. Now if God so clothes the grass of the field, which today is, and tomorrow is thrown into the oven, will He not much more clothe you, O you of little faith?
>
> Therefore do not worry, saying, "What shall we eat?" or "What shall we drink?" or "What shall we wear?" For after all these things the Gentiles seek. For your heavenly Father knows that you need all these things. *But seek first the kingdom of God and His righteousness, and all these things shall be added to you.* Therefore do not worry about tomorrow, for

> tomorrow will worry about its own things. Sufficient for the day is its own trouble.
>
> —NKJV, EMPHASIS ADDED

God even gave us provision to buy our first home, giving us a down payment in a providential way. We became more and more confident that everything we own belongs to God, and if we follow His lead, He will never fail to amaze.

An Unexpected Birthday Gift

God still stretches us in giving. Not long ago I met a woman named Pam at a dinner for a nonprofit ministry I volunteered to help. She mentioned that she played guitar. In the days that followed, the Lord led me to pray for Pam. Then He told me to give her my new favorite guitar, a Paul Reed Smith. This guitar was special because I handpicked it after months of searching. Its tone was beautiful, and it was blood red, reminding me of the blood Jesus shed for me. Not wanting to give it up, I tried to ignore what He was telling me. But when the Lord really wants me to do something, He makes me restless. I began losing sleep over it, so I stopped delaying, packed the guitar in its case, and prepared to ship it to Pam.

"Overnight," the Lord said. "Ship it to her overnight."

"But that costs so much more!" I complained. "You already told me to give away my new favorite guitar. Now You're charging me more for it?"

Not wanting to lose any more sleep, I obeyed and shipped it overnight to Pam, who lived on the West Coast. Soon it became clear why there was such urgency.

The day after I shipped it, Pam called.

"Do you know what you did?" she said through tears.

"Yes," I said. "I sent you a very good guitar." I didn't want to squash her moment by telling her how much I loved it.

"But do you know what you did?" she asked again.

I didn't get it. "No," I said.

"You shipped it FedEx to arrive on this day," she said.

"He told me I had to," I said, feeling the sting in my wallet again.

"Today is my birthday!" she said. Instantly I began tearing up as well. The Lord loved her so much that He insisted the guitar arrive for her birthday. Because I had delayed in shipping it, He made me send it overnight to arrive on the right day. Pam also told me it was the exact guitar she had always wanted. When I hung up, I felt like a million bucks, though all I had done was give away a guitar. Knowing I had participated with the Father in giving this gift was worth a thousand guitars. As always, giving reminded me of Jesus's gift to me of eternal life. To be like Him in giving is a wonderful privilege. He had shown me again that you never know how He will use our giving to change someone's life.

Learning to surrender our bank account taught us to rely on God, a lesson that He would put to use in other areas of our lives. Every time we give something, God blesses us with something better. More importantly, God taught us to be faithful with "little" so He could trust us with more. For me, that "more" meant an unfolding gift of prophecy that I didn't realize I had.

It also meant that the enemy would try to wreck my calling before I even discovered it.

Chapter 5

SHIPWRECKED: HOW "PROPHECY" NEARLY BURNED US

THE FIRST TIME I ever prophesied was at a Michael Sweet concert in the summer of 2001, and I didn't even know what was happening. My plan was to unwind after a hard workweek by seeing one of my favorite musicians perform. God's plan was to give me a glimpse of a new way to walk by the Spirit.

I had been a diehard Stryper fan as a teenager. The band, founded by brothers Michael and Robert Sweet, played heavy metal Christian music back when nobody else did. When Stryper disbanded in the early 1990s, I was heartbroken, but a decade later Michael Sweet released a solo album called *Truth* and was on tour to promote it. I saw he was playing at a club on Long Island, about an hour from my office in Manhattan, and Vicki and I agreed that a night out would do me good.

I headed to the venue straight from work and got there early, around four o'clock. The website didn't say when the concert would start, and the door was open, so I walked in and heard the band doing a sound check. Quietly

I grabbed a seat to enjoy it. What a thrill to get an up-close view of Michael, a guy who had influenced my life so much. Bass player Tracy Ferrie was jumping around, joking with the other band members and enjoying himself. It was great to watch their fun interactions.

After the sound check, I was stunned when Michael came over to my table and sat down.

"How are you doing?" he asked.

"I—I'm doing OK," I replied, fumbling for words. I had never met a famous person before. "The band sounded great," I continued. "Can I take you guys out to dinner?"

"What am I thinking?" I asked myself.

"That would be cool," he said, and a few minutes later I was in the van with the band. I could not believe what was happening.

We went to a hamburger place and had a great time together, then jumped in the van and headed back to the club. When we walked in, an opening act was onstage playing. Michael and the guys went downstairs, but I hesitated, wondering if I should follow or join the audience. The bouncer motioned me to a seat on the side of the stage. "Having dinner with Michael Sweet and watching the show from onstage—could it get any better?" I wondered.

Better and definitely weirder.

After a few minutes Tracy Ferrie came back upstairs, walked by me and said hi, then sat in a chair in front of me to watch the opening band. A few moments later I felt a stirring inside me—my stomach turned as if I'd eaten something bad. I tried to ignore it, but the stirring became more intense. "I can't be getting sick now!" I thought. Then another urge came upon me, an urge to go sit by Tracy. "Why do that?" I thought. "Am I just being a superfan? There's no way I'm going to annoy this guy before a show."

As I tried to make sense of what I felt, Tracy turned and motioned me over to him. Surprised, I got up and sat in the chair next to him.

"So what's your story?" he asked me.

I had no idea what to say.

"My name is Hubie," was what came out, and then something strange and totally unexpected happened. Words began flowing from my mouth without any help from my mind. Startled and perplexed by what was happening, I knew I was speaking but didn't even know what I was saying. It seemed to go on for a very long time in some kind of slow motion. After my mouth stopped, Tracy turned to me. His eyes were swollen with tears.

"Thank you," he said. "I really needed to hear that! You don't know what it means to me."

"OK," I replied, not knowing what had just happened and probably more surprised than he was. He thanked me again, looked at his watch, said "Gotta go," and disappeared downstairs.

"What was that all about?" I thought as I went back to my original chair. The experience was scary at first but left me feeling peaceful. My stomach was now completely calm. The indigestion had gone away. *How strange!*

Tracy came back upstairs.

"Come with me," he said, motioning with his hand.

I followed him downstairs and found the band in an underground room. Michael turned to me.

"The club doesn't want to pay us until after the show, and that wasn't the agreement," he said. "If we wait until after the show, there is a good chance we won't get paid. The owner is in the next room. What should we do?"

Michael Sweet was asking my advice? What on earth? I weighed in as best I could.

"I would go up to the microphone and say the club doesn't want to pay us and sorry, but we are leaving."

Michael winced. He really didn't want to do that.

"Why don't we pray about it?" Tracy suggested, so we all joined hands and lifted the situation up to God. No sooner had we finished and let go of one another's hands than the club owner walked into the room and handed Michael the money. We looked at one another like, "Can you believe this?"

Back upstairs, the band put on a great show that night. Afterward I went to the van to say good-bye before heading home.

"Are you an angel?" Tracy asked.

I laughed. "No, I am not."

"Then are you a pastor?" he asked.

"No, I am not a pastor either," I said. "I am a believer and just came to see the show."

We prayed a quick prayer, and they headed out to their next show. I drove home, trying to make sense of the strange encounter with Tracy, the openness of the band to my presence, and my stomach's sudden churning and equally sudden stop. "Must have been a one-time thing," I concluded.

Repeat Performance

A few months later, on a missionary trip to Sweden, it happened again. At the end of a service I was praying for a woman when something seemed to come over me and words flowed out of my mouth beyond my control. It was like praying in tongues, but the words were in English. I could hear the woman sobbing, and I kept my head down and let the words continue. I didn't know what I was saying, but it had a dramatic effect on her. After I finished, she looked at me with red, swollen eyes and asked, "How did you know?" All I could think to say was, "The Lord knows all."

Once again, I didn't know what to make of it, but since it seemed to help the woman, I decided it was a good thing. I left it at that and didn't think about it again.

Meanwhile, I had exchanged e-mails with Michael Sweet and Tracy Ferrie after the concert and prayed for them a lot over the next few months. One day as I was praying for Michael, I felt the urge to write something down and send it to him. I e-mailed him what I had gotten but received no reply and felt foolish. "What a dumb thing to do, bothering a guy like that," I thought. "I'm not doing that again." But when I prayed for Michael again, the urge came back. "No way," I said to myself. "I'm not sending him another e-mail."

Restless sleep hounded me. "Too much coffee," I thought. The next day I cut down on caffeine, but my sleep got worse. After a few nights tossing and turning, the urge to send the e-mail grew stronger. I relented, hoping it was the Holy Spirit, and sent Michael another e-mail. Again, no answer. "I can't believe I made the same mistake twice," I thought, feeling like an idiot. "How could I face this guy if I ever saw him again?"

Doubly determined never to e-mail Michael again, I steeled myself against the possibility. Yet the Holy Spirit kept prompting me to continue. When I sat at the computer to write the e-mails, words would just flow. I didn't want to send him messages, especially since I was getting no response and was beginning to doubt my own sanity. But God was using it to bring about a divine connection that would prove pivotal in our lives.

Apparently Michael's late wife, Kyle Sweet, was reading

the e-mails. She asked her good friend and former manager of Stryper, Daryn Hinton (a woman), why Daryn had told me certain private things that I had mentioned in my e-mails. Daryn told Kyle she had no idea who I was or how I knew what I knew. Piqued and determined to get to the bottom of the matter, Daryn e-mailed me and introduced herself as the former manager of Stryper. We traded e-mails for a few months, and one day she informed me that she was coming to New York City with her friend Patty Gannon to meet me. I did not realize it, but God was sending these two women to introduce us to a new way of life and a deeper obedience in being led by the Spirit of God, a level of surrender I never even dreamed of.

We met at a Thai restaurant near my office, and Daryn and Patty gave me the warmest greeting. There was something special about these two women that I had not seen in other believers. The love of Christ emanated from them. We chatted about Michael's solo album and other things. They also talked about the early days of Stryper and the miracles that happened. Excitement danced in their eyes as they shared about these supernatural experiences. I didn't know how to categorize what they told me because I thought miracles happened only during "special" occasions like missionary trips, crusades, or in church services. They took it for granted that supernatural stuff could happen anytime, anyplace.

Finally I couldn't resist asking, "Why are you here? Why did you fly to New York from California?"

They both answered, "To meet you!"

What? This made no sense. Flying cross-country to meet an accountant? Daryn added, "The Lord told us to come and meet you in person." I almost couldn't believe it. Who would fly three thousand miles to meet one person because the Lord told them to? Yet they treated it as perfectly normal. They didn't even know why God told them to come, and I don't think it mattered to them. Obedience was their only goal.

We said good night, and I felt I had known them for years. Over the next months all the stories they had shared about God moving supernaturally rolled around in my mind.

"Are these people for real?" I thought. "Is this how God wants His followers to live? Are Daryn and Patty the exception or the rule?"

We kept in contact through e-mail and an occasional phone call. The next year Daryn called to say the Lord had told her and Patty to come back to New York City to meet me again. She and Patty stayed at our home, and when they came through our door, joy and love seemed to billow into the room. That night they shared in depth about how Stryper got started and how the Lord opened one door after another for the band. I was amazed by their stories, and after a while I posed the same question I did during their first visit: "Why did you come to New York City again?"

They replied unhelpfully, "The Lord told us to."

"You just bought airline tickets, packed up, and came?" I clarified. They nodded.

"I can't imagine doing that," I thought, little knowing what lay ahead for Vicki and me.

I remained perplexed and a little irritated by their lifestyle of radical obedience.

The following year Stryper reformed, and Daryn and Patti visited us again. We all went to see Stryper perform in Asbury Park, New Jersey. After parking the cars, Patty said, "I need a few minutes." She began wandering through the parking lot, weaving between cars apparently aimlessly. I watched the strange ritual.

"She does that," Daryn said.

"Does what?" I asked.

"Walks around and prays for all the people coming and also for the show, so the Lord will have His way tonight."

"Really?" I wondered. "Prayer in church or a ministry setting I understand, but out here in a parking lot? This is no place for ministry."

I had no idea how I would eat those words.

Daryn and Patty spent the next few days with us, and Vicki and I were fascinated by their lifestyle and drawn to the fire in their eyes. They seemed carefree and full of love all the time, not just at church. I still couldn't get my head around the fact that they flew wherever God told them without knowing why.

Seeds of change were planted in our hearts. For the first time in my life I realized it was OK not to be like everyone else. I could be the individual God created me to be, and if that made me different as it did Daryn and Patty, that was fine. Deep inside I wanted to be led by His Spirit and knew it would require a greater level of obedience and trust. The sense of adventure and purpose and risk captured my imagination. It also made my life look pale and boring by comparison. "Do people even know God is in my life by the way I carry myself?" I wondered. "Can they see that I am different? Or am I just one of the millions of people doing life the safe, familiar way?"

The faith-filled life came alive to me in the account of Jesus and Peter walking on the sea. Peter had to put aside his fears, stand against worldly thinking, and keep his eyes focused on Jesus when he stepped out of the boat. Peter walked on the water for no other reason than Jesus commanded him to come. Jesus was in complete control of the situation, including the wind and the waves. When Jesus commands us to come, we too can do it with confidence.

Then, just as Vicki and I were being stirred spiritually, the enemy tried to cut us off from our destiny.

Guided by Prophetic Words

The first prophecy I ever received given in the early 1990s at a church we were visiting for the first time. After worship one evening we sat down, and one of the deacons got up to speak. I was restless, troubled by an invitation I had received for the coming Friday. A good friend was getting married and having a bachelor party. I was the only married guy scheduled to attend, and they were planning things that a faithful, married person shouldn't be part of.

Deacon Sam stopped, paused for a moment, and then said, "I don't know what it is, but somebody here is planning on doing something they know they shouldn't do." Everyone glanced around to see whom he might be talking about. Sam continued, "It's not right what they're planning, but you're going to do it anyway."

"That's so vague," I thought. "He could be describing anyone."

He kept going. "You know you shouldn't do it, and you have many reservations, but you plan to do it anyway. The Lord wants you to know you are not going to look at it the same way again, and He's calling you. He wants you to know that you know what's right and what's wrong." I knew by now that this word was about me. I acted like it was for someone else, but I was wearing the bull's-eye on my chest. It was the first time I had received a word, and it was so accurate that I was intrigued by this kind of supernatural communication.

At this church the only members permitted to prophesy were the pastor, elders, deacons, ministers, and the "prophet of the house." Over the next couple of years I received a few more prophecies, and they were accurate as well, so Vicki and I began to rely on prophecy as a normal part of our Christian lives. The meaning of the messages always seemed coded, but clear enough for us to understand.

Vicki and I started to make decisions based on prophecies we received, mainly from the pastor of this church. This person had been accurate before, so we trusted whatever the pastor said. We didn't realize we were neglecting the instruction to test the spirits (1 John 4:1–6) and to test prophecies and hold to the good. We believed the pastor heard from God and gave accurate answers from God. We began to go to the pastor to ask for prayer for problems and let the pastor's answers determine our decisions. This approach seemed to work for a time.

Then three incidents occurred in rapid succession that left us feeling devastated.

The first happened when Vicki was pregnant with our fourth child. One Sunday at the church, when Vicki was approaching the end of the first trimester, the pastor called us up to the altar and prayed over us and the baby in Vicki's womb. The pastor said the baby would be healthy, a joy to us, and was being called by God for a specific purpose. It was a beautiful word, and I was happy about it. Later in the week Vicki got another word from the "prophet of the house," which confirmed what the pastor had said.

A few weeks later Vicki got cramps and started to bleed lightly. I could see fear creeping in, so I stood on the prophetic word and said to her, "The baby got a couple of words, and I am totally relying on them. Nothing bad is going to happen." I was convinced of it.

The cramps and bleeding worsened. "I have a really bad feeling about this," Vicki said. "Don't worry," I said. "Everything is going to be fine." But she was pale and I began to wonder, "Is this happening to us? Is this real?"

The situation did not improve. A little while later Vicki came downstairs from the bathroom. "I think I just lost the baby," she said. I was blindsided. "We are walking with God in obedience," I thought. "How could this happen? What about the two prophecies that the baby would be healthy?"

Dazed and wounded by Vicki's miscarriage, we tried to make sense of it all over the ensuing weeks.

At this same time our seven-year-old son, Daniel, became very sick with severe eczema, a skin condition. Doctors told us it was the worst case they had ever seen. His skin cracked open all over his body and fluid oozed out. It was scary to look at. Even water felt like fire on his skin and made him scream in pain. Nearly everything he came into contact with caused the eczema to flare up and made his skin turn as red as a fire truck. Our hearts broke to see him suffer.

We cried out to God for Daniel to be healed and brought him up to the altar for prayer every Sunday. One Sunday while we were at the same church where we had received the prophecy about our unborn baby, one of the ministers prayed for Daniel and instructed us to soak him in ocean salt water three times, then apply Lysol to kill the infection, and he would be healed. The minister said the rash was a fungus and Lysol would kill it. The advice sounded crazy to me. I told Vicki we could try the salt water but were definitely not putting Lysol on his skin. Back home I made a weak saltwater solution and put a couple of drops on Daniel's arm. The solution burned his skin, so I quickly rinsed it off. "What was this minister thinking?" I wondered, and the faulty counsel added to our mounting disappointment.

Soon after that, a ministry opportunity presented itself in Texas. We felt strongly that God wanted us to go but were very concerned about Daniel's ability to travel long distances. We asked the pastor for counsel, and the answer was that we should go and call daily for prayer. We left for Texas believing God would keep Daniel free of a flare-up of eczema on the trip.

When we got to Texas, Daniel had a very bad flare-up that required a visit to the emergency room. The doctor who treated him was so ignorant that he kept leaving the room and returning with new information, as if stepping outside to read a medical book. I knew more about eczema than he did. His last comment was, "Well, you know there's no cure." Since we were on the road, Vicki and I felt we had no choice but to go with the doctor's recommendation to give Daniel steroids to calm the flare-up. We knew the steroids would give only temporary relief.

The relief was indeed short-lived. We headed to Florida for a vacation at Disney World, a place we had long dreamed of visiting as a family. Daniel's skin flared up so badly that we couldn't even go. We badly needed rejuvenation as a family after Vicki's miscarriage and the ongoing problems with Daniel's skin. Now we were stuck in a hotel in Florida with our son suffering night and day.

God showed compassion on us through a wonderful couple I knew through a ministry I served as an accountant. They saw we were frustrated and put us up at a lavish beach club in Boca Raton. Their act of kindness ministered deeply to me and opened my eyes to the kind of person I wanted to be. It also saved our vacation from becoming a total disaster.

Back in New York, Daniel again had to go to the emergency room. His body had retained so much water that his legs looked like an elephant's. The doctor gave him steroids to calm the eczema for a couple of weeks. These steroid shots made his skin look completely normal. We knew the eczema would flare back up with a vengeance once the steroids wore off.

We told the pastor everything that happened. That Sunday at church the pastor dropped a bomb on us. Calling us to the front, the pastor instructed Vicki and me to stand facing the congregation, me on the left, Vicki on the right, and the pastor in the middle.

"I told them not to go, but they didn't listen and went anyway," the pastor said, implying that we had been rebellious. Then the pastor recounted to the congregation all the bad things that had happened during the trip. Vicki and I stood there dumbfounded. Was this really happening?

Finally, the pastor called Daniel to the front and showed everyone his arms. "Despite what the parents did, God is faithful. Look what the Lord has done! Daniel has been healed!" Vicki and I nearly fainted. He looked "healed" because he had taken steroids, but the eczema was going to flare up again in a few days. We walked back to our seats in a daze. Why did the pastor confirm to us that God wanted us to go on this trip and then tell the congregation that we disobeyed? How could the pastor declare Daniel was healed after we had explained that he was on steroids? I kept shaking my head in disbelief.

The third incident had happened a little earlier and involved a house we were thinking of buying in New

Jersey. We had asked the pastor to pray about it, and the pastor and an elder had driven out to see it. The pastor had prayed and affirmed that it was the house God had for us. A few days later, the house was sold to another family through no fault of our own.

The house…the baby…Daniel's situation—all of it happened within a few months, and the prophecies about each had been wildly inaccurate. Vicki and I decided we could no longer attend that church. Our confidence in the leadership and in the gifts that operated there was shattered. Wounded, confused, and disillusioned, we lost some friends because of our decision. Worse, we began to doubt our ability to hear from God. "Are the gifts of the Spirit true or false?" we asked. "What is of God and what is of the enemy? What can we believe and whom can we trust?" We weren't sure anymore.

FORGIVENESS AND HEALING

We quit going to church for a while and watched church services on TV, but it didn't compare to the life we had found in the gathering of believers. Then one day we received a phone call from our dear friend Charles Murray.

"You know, you have been shipwrecked," he said. He meant we felt isolated, alone. At last, someone related to how we were feeling. Charles sent us the book *The Bait of Satan* by John Bevere, which showed us we needed to forgive those we felt had hurt us. We started to attend the church Charles was attending and discovered other people who had left the church where we had received the inaccurate words. All of us had been spiritually and emotionally wounded, but none of us wanted to abandon our faith as some had. Together we went through healing, sharing our hearts, praying for and comforting one another. Sometimes Vicki would start weeping during the church service for no apparent reason. It was like our spirits were being cleansed of wounds.

As for prophecy and the other gifts of the Spirit, I had seen enough for a while. Prophecy had indeed helped us on many occasions. It brought encouragement, hope, direction, and warning. It demonstrated the personal nature of God. But false prophecy had turned our hearts away from the gifts, at least for the time being.

Years later I was with a man named John Paul Jackson, who led a well-established prophetic ministry. I shared about this experience and John Paul told me, "Right when your gift was ready to start, that's when all these false prophecies started happening. The enemy tried to sabotage you, but you made your way back."

He was right. Eventually we started serving in local church ministry again, and the joy of the Lord was restored to us. But God had one more season of great difficulty to test our mettle before launching me into my prophetic ministry calling.

Chapter 6

YES TO THE RADICAL LIFE

SOMETIMES YOU GET hit by a perfect storm, and sometimes that storm comes from God.

After leaving the church where we had been so wounded, Vicki and I turned our attention to family. We were done with ministry for a while. The best thing, we felt, was to raise our kids and provide a stable home for them financially. Vicki had returned to work with great favor from the Lord, and we both were at high points in our careers. By the world's standards we had it all. So it was a total surprise when God asked us, once again, to give it all up.

I had closed my CPA practice a few months earlier in favor of a new challenge. A decade as a CPA in Manhattan had left me burned out. The volume of work, the pressure of the decisions, paying salaries and benefits to my employees, and the many hours interacting with each client overwhelmed my mind and emotions. My blood pressure went sky high and wouldn't come down even with medication. I felt I was wasting away, working hard to take a couple of days off, then working like crazy to catch back up. I was always behind the eight ball to manage cash flow and advise people's businesses.

When the opportunity came to work full time for a

client as their chief financial officer, I jumped at it. I gave my old business to a faithful employee and began a new phase of my career working for an up-and-coming fashion company that designed couture evening gowns for celebrities and was expanding into the home furnishings accessory market. I loved the people and felt energized by the artistic side of the business. Plus, it was exciting to be part of something that was growing so quickly. When I started, there were six people and a shipping guy. A year and a half later there were fifteen of us.

God did tremendous things, helping us get into trade shows, magazines, and major department stores. People thought I was calm and cool. They didn't know I would close the door and pray like crazy that we would make the right decisions. All day long we were working with overseas factories that produced our growing line of products. I was so pressed for time that when my son Daniel needed help with homework, I did it via a conference call from the office.

Vicki had renewed her ambitions of climbing the corporate ladder as well, and her identity became more and more tied to her job. But there was a price to pay. Home life was suffering.

Vicki and I were growing apart, and we fought more or less constantly.

"Daddy, you know it has been about a year since we ate together as a family," my daughter Sara informed me one day. It hurt to hear that—and hurt even more that she had been paying attention. I loved what I was doing, and work commanded most of my attention. Family bonds and personal relationships were deteriorating fast. Although comfortable from a financial perspective, we were stressed out and just plain unhappy. I felt run-down all the time, just like when I was a CPA. We were getting ill pretty much all the time. Memories of my dysfunctional childhood haunted my mind. "I'm the head of my family," I thought, "yet here I am creating the kind of unhealthy home I never wanted and becoming the person I promised not to be."

Spiritually we were in a drought, the lowest of lows in our walk with the Lord. In the aftermath of leaving our church we put our jobs ahead of God and ahead of family life. We went through the motions of family and ministry but felt completely spent mentally, physically, and spiritually. The money was there, but I asked God, "Is this all there is? Where is the fulfillment and purpose in life?" The experiences He had given me after the Michael Sweet concert had gone dormant. I appreciated the example of Patty and Daryn, but several years had passed, and those lessons were a world away.

I see now that God allowed us to have our dream jobs to show us that the worldly success, status, and financial stability we desired did not bring lasting fulfillment. Our priorities had to get in order. We were on a merry-go-round and didn't know how to get off.

One night in desperation Vicki and I cried out to God. We told Him we would make any change He wanted for things to get better. Certain Bible verses convicted us:

> Then Jesus said to His disciples, "If anyone will come after Me, let him deny himself, and take up his cross, and follow Me. For whoever would save his life will lose it, and whoever loses his life for My sake will find it."
>
> —Matthew 16:24–25

> Do not store up for yourselves treasures on earth where moth and rust destroy and where thieves break in and steal. But store up for yourselves treasures in heaven, where neither moth nor rust destroy and where thieves do not break in nor steal, for where your treasure is, there will your heart be also.... No one can serve two masters. For either he will hate the one and love the other, or else he will hold to the one and despise the other. You cannot serve God and money.
>
> —MATTHEW 6:19–21, 24

Weary, discontented, and disillusioned, we knew our lives were way out of sync with God's plan. I remember our exact prayer: "Lord, do whatever You need to make things better." We didn't know how swift and jarring His response would be.

JUMPING OFF THE MERRY-GO-ROUND

At work one Saturday I was tending to business when the Lord gave me one of those life experiences you don't see coming. All of a sudden I felt the curtains pulled back from my eyes. I looked out my window and saw sunshine as if for the first time. Peace flooded my office, and my mind was so relaxed and clear. He began to show me how my priorities had changed over the past year. The reality of my life was not pretty; then again, it was such a peaceful feeling to see reality for what it was.

"What is more important to you?" the Lord asked me. I knew where this conversation was going. A few minutes later He told me very firmly, "It is time to leave your job."

"Give up my dream job that I love so much? The job

makes me feel so important and worth something. My identity is in this job!"

I stared out the window and knew I had to quit. Fulfillment at work didn't last. One day I was excited about getting into a trade show or a magazine; the next day it was business as usual. The joy of each accomplishment faded fast.

As the day went on, His peace grew in me, and by the end of the day I had one foot out the door. Driving home I experienced His peace as I hadn't in years. How Vicki would take the news, I didn't know; but God wanted me to do this. As I walked into my home, a strange sensation engulfed me—joy. There were my beautiful wife and wonderful kids. Taking a deep breath, I approached Vicki.

"The Lord told me to quit my job," I said.

She looked at me and said, "Yes, you should."

Whew! That was easy.

The next day at work I resigned and came home with the company as an accounting client as they had been before. Still, our income went down—way down. I felt I was on a roller coaster just before a steep drop. You're pretty sure it's safe, but you never really know. How God would give us income was a huge question mark.

The next shock came the day our fourth child was born. After Vicki's miscarriage, God had blessed us with another son, Paul. I was driving home from the hospital praising God for the birth of Paul, our "final" child, when I heard the Holy Spirit tell me clearly, "You're not done yet. There is another one."

"But Lord, You don't understand. We are so done!" I responded.

Overwhelmed by the idea of raising and providing for

another child, I was depressed by the time I got home. Vicki noticed I wasn't myself.

"Just a lot on my mind with work," I said. No way was I telling her what the Holy Spirit told me. I figured, if He wanted her to have another baby, He'd have to tell her Himself.

Days passed, and Vicki again inquired about my downbeat mood. I gave the same answer: "Work." This went on for a few weeks. Finally she cornered me and looked deep into my eyes as if reading what was there. She didn't like what she saw.

"We are not having another child!" she said.

I hadn't said a thing. I stood there in stunned surprise.

"You must be hearing incorrectly from God," she continued, and I was willing to agree with her. Why would He want us to have another baby at middle age? Weren't four children enough?

The next thing I knew, Vicki was campaigning to have me "fixed." She wanted to seal the deal for good. The kids heard her talking about it, and it became the topic of the house.

"Mommy wants to get you neutered?" my daughter Kristin asked me one day, and I cringed at the thought of the procedure. Plus, I knew the Holy Spirit had spoken to me. Whenever I tried to let go of the idea of a fifth child, it came back like a playful puppy.

Vicki's opposition was relentless, and I failed to persuade her, so one day I put the decision on her.

"OK, you win," I said. "I'll get fixed, but if we were supposed to have another child in God's perfect will, then it's on your head, not mine. I wash my hands of it. Now, you tell me when my procedure is and I'll be there."

Vicki went a little pale. She quit bugging me about it, and I knew she was seeking God's will in private.

Miriam Joy

God had given me the names for our first four children, so I assumed He would give me the name of our last child, the one Vicki still didn't think we were having. During my prayer time one day the Holy Spirit spoke a name to me: *Miriam Joy.* I loved the name and now knew we were having a girl. I was beside myself with happiness.

Vicki's opposition to a fifth child crumbled with the arrival of an unexpected prophetic word. One Sunday morning during church we were writing notes to each other in the little notebook where Vicki takes notes on the messages. I wrote down, "If God wants us to have a child, why do you see it as such a burden?" Vicki responded by listing all kinds of excuses: "What will other people say? We're already forty-one years old. We have four children and no finances."

Suddenly the speaker called out, "And Sister Vicki." We froze, feeling like we had been caught not paying attention. Then the speaker, a woman, started prophesying over Vicki: "You are like the Shulamite woman—you don't ask God for anything. This is what God is going to do with you: He's going to give you a son, and after you have your son, He will bring you to your destiny." By the time she finished, Vicki was on the floor sobbing, overcome by the Spirit. The speaker picked up where she had left off and finished her message.

It's funny how you try to reason things out based on the knowledge you have. I knew from the Holy Spirit that we were having a daughter named Miriam Joy, not a son, and had shared this with Vicki. While driving home, we puzzled our way through the word: "When the speaker talked about us having a son, maybe it was an analogy that we are 'pregnant' in the spirit and about to birth something spiritually." Only later did we realize what her word meant.

The Holy Spirit's conviction grew so strong on Vicki that she was unable to sleep at night. She finally surrendered to the Lord and agreed to have another child. The Lord began to share with us very clearly that the baby had a purpose and that we were the chosen vessels to bring this child into the world. Who were we to say no?

Then He shocked us again. A month after the baby was conceived, God told Vicki to quit her job again. That meant losing her income, her health benefits, and our last bit of financial security.

"Lord, how could You ask us to have another child and make both of us quit our jobs again?" we asked in prayer. "Don't You know we have four mouths to feed, two mortgages, and two car payments?" We pleaded with Him to relent, but nothing swayed Him.

Like me, Vicki's life had been wrapped up in her career. Quitting meant a loss of personal identity, the death of a certain self-image. Two things ministered to her in those days. One was Mary's response to the angel who had just announced God's plan for her to conceive the Christ child. Luke 1:38 records Mary's response: "Behold the maidservant of the Lord! Let it be to me according to your word" (NKJV). It's amazing how one simple verse can embolden your faith so much. Vicki held to that example like it was a life preserver. *Let it be to me according to your word.*

The other encouragement came from a song by Hillsong artist Miriam Webster. The song, "Exceeding Joy," says we find exceeding joy when we answer Jesus's call.

The words of that song encouraged us both on many a fearful night.

Criticism and even ridicule poured in from family and friends. "You're irresponsible," they said to our faces and behind our backs. "You have children to support and lives to lead. How can you quit your jobs? What are you doing with your lives? You'll lose everything." It looked like they might be right. Our household income plummeted to a third of what it had been. I threw my hands up and told God, "This just doesn't add up. How am I to make ends meet?" Stripped of the ability to provide for my family, I felt inadequate as a father. Some days I couldn't help but feel despondent. Life was hard, and so was holding on to the promise.

For months things got worse. We depleted our savings and retirement money to pay bills. We canceled our health insurance policy because we could no longer afford the monthly premiums. Two weeks later Paul ended up in intensive care with complications from an RSV infection that restricted his breathing. I sat by as my son lay in a hospital bed hooked up to tubes and machines. Doctors came and went, checking vital signs and whispering to each other about his condition.

"God, heal our little boy," we prayed almost constantly, bombarding heaven with prayers for Paul. But we had information the doctors didn't: the Holy Spirit had spoken to us two weeks earlier, "Your son is no longer sick." At the time we had absolutely no idea what this meant and to which one of our sons He was referring. When Paul went to the ICU, we realized the prophecy was about him, given to us by God so we could hold on to hope and stand against this spiritual attack.

God was faithful to His word, and Paul's breathing miraculously improved just when doctors predicted he would need a breathing tube inserted in his throat. Paul was released from the hospital just in time for Thanksgiving, and despite our incredibly shrinking bank account, we felt more thankful than we had in years.

Our focus turned to Vicki and her pregnancy with our

fifth child, a girl we would name Miriam Joy. We prayed daily for Miriam Joy's health; her calling; her ability to hear clearly from God; her protection, destiny, healing, and everything else we could think of. On the day of the sonogram I woke up happy and eager to see my new daughter. We went to the clinic and the technician asked if we wanted to know the sex of the baby.

"Of course," I replied, smiling because we knew already. It was a good thing I was sitting down.

"It's a baby boy!" the technician announced.

I could not have been more unprepared.

"What? Are you sure?" Vicki and I asked. "Can you check again?"

The technician replied, "Yes, I am sure the baby is a boy. Here, look at the screen."

A wonderful moment turned into a massive "Huh?" An unwelcome lump formed in my throat. "This must be one of the biggest mistakes of my life," I thought, my confidence badly shaken. "This calls into question everything we're hearing, all the risks we're taking financially. Maybe our friends are right. Maybe we are completely crazy."

Once again we felt burned by a "prophecy" that did not come true. We couldn't help feeling wounded and confused all over again.

But God was using every moment of that pregnancy experience to graduate us to new levels of faith. One lesson involved Vicki's miraculous healing from a sickness rooted in unresolved issues with her father. Vicki had developed gestational diabetes during her fourth pregnancy and developed it again during her fifth. She failed a glucose intolerance test. Frustrated that God would not deliver her from it, I remembered meeting a minister named Caspar McCloud who was knowledgeable about the spiritual roots of disease. We received ministry and prayer from Caspar one evening by phone.

"Let me ask you, Vicki, have you suffered from abandonment and a broken relationship with your father?" he said. Vicki's mouth nearly hit the floor. How could he have known that? Could that really be the cause of the diabetes instead of hormonal imbalance as the doctor had suggested? Vicki went through prayer steps to forgive her father, receive her heavenly Father's love, and receive healing.

To our amazement, her symptoms disappeared immediately after the phone call. She took a glucose intolerance test the next day and passed it! Doctors say that gestational diabetes goes away once a woman gives birth and her hormones return to normal, but not during pregnancy. God was healing Vicki's body and soul and showing He was with us.

Vicki's other major lesson came through a television show. Giving up her career had been tough. Vicki likes to tackle challenges, learn new things, and stay busy. She feared boredom at home and rued the loss of mental challenge. Our financial situation weighed on us too, and we were already falling behind on all our bills. Vicki would wake up in the morning, look out the window, and wonder, "Is this the last day in our home? How much harder is it going to get once the baby arrives?" Daily devotions turned into sob sessions, and she repented often for being afraid.

God was faithful to lead her to Sid Roth's website, which has hundreds of episodes of his show, *It's Supernatural!* The show features testimonies of provision, deliverance, healing, and revelation from believers from all walks of life. Vicki's spirit soared as she watched countless episodes. She claimed the promises and miraculous works God performed for these people and prayed with greater expectation to receive all He had planned for us. Through Sid's show God taught her how to encourage and strengthen herself in the Lord. It even gave her the boldness to obey the Holy Spirit and start a Bible study in our home. A small group of women from local churches gathered every Friday morning to worship and study the Word with powerful results. They experienced emotional and physical healing and breakthroughs in relationships. Sid Roth's encouraging and faith-imparting interviews strengthened our home, and we were grateful.

By the time our fifth child was ready to be born, Vicki was like a new woman. She had told God she wanted to grow in faith by claiming and receiving a painless birthing experience, like the woman who had written the book *Supernatural Childbirth*. Vicki brought a CD player to the hospital and played praise and worship music in the labor and delivery rooms. We declared God's promises out loud the entire time. Everything happened peacefully and without pain. The sense of God's presence in the room was strong. So our son was born, and we named him Michael. He came into the world so calmly that he didn't even cry. The doctors and nurses thought we were crazy but couldn't deny that our approach worked. Vicki, "the singing pregnant woman," became the talk of the nurses' station.

Michael brought us great joy, but Vicki and I still struggled to make sense of the "Miriam Joy" word. I was sure I had heard God wrong.

UNABLE TO MOVE

Our finances were still pretty rocky, and we basically lived day by day. We literally felt like the Israelites wandering around the desert being fed by the hand of God.

The Lord showed us we didn't need jobs as a crutch for our confidence but should trust Him entirely. We thought we had been trusting Him entirely before, but we really hadn't been. He even provided a new tenant to rent our second home. In fact, three families bid against each other to rent the home, even though the market was soft at the time. One family offered to prepay an entire year's rent. We accepted that offer, which provided much-needed money for bills.

By this time Vicki and I were talking openly about moving to another state so we could start over. We had our eyes at different times on Washington state, Georgia, Maryland, and Florida, where some of our friends lived. Each was more family friendly and had a lower cost of living than New Jersey. But when we tried to move, God slammed the doors shut. At one point we had our house for sale, but after several months there were no buyers.

One day I was talking on the phone with Wendy, a friend in ministry with a prophetic gift. We were discussing her financial matters when she stopped midsentence and said, "I don't know what this means, but God said you're not supposed to move to Florida." Then she picked up where she left off. Wendy had no idea we were trying to relocate, so I was taken aback by the experience. Disappointed, Vicki and I took the house off the market and set aside our own desires for God's.

A few weeks later Vicki was driving home from the grocery store and experienced an overwhelming peace as God spoke to her spirit, "If you will trust Me to stay in New Jersey, I will show you that I will provide for your needs." To our amazement, for the next twelve months God sent people to unexpectedly give us cash every month as a sign of His faithfulness and to assure us we had heard correctly to stay.

Then my phone started ringing, old clients calling out of the blue to ask if I would take them back. How some of them found out I was available, I will never know. I did almost nothing to rebuild my practice, but God rebuilt it for me. I was so reluctant to do accounting again that I refused to make business cards. To be truthful, I did not want to be a CPA again, but it was not about me anymore. The Lord had a purpose in it, and I would soon watch Him use accounting to bring me into divine appointments.

For six years we lived on the brink of financial ruin while God provided our daily needs and never let us go under. Quitting our dream jobs meant real financial loss but great spiritual gain during that transformative time. We saw His faithfulness many times through supernatural provision as He taught us to live by the principle of daily bread. He also shut down our attempts to relocate, demonstrating that He cared where we lived and had a path for us, which was encouraging. We also learned to endure criticism from people who didn't understand our new lifestyle.

Mostly we learned that doing great exploits for Christ means counting the cost, denying ourselves, and keeping a pure heart toward God. It was not our place to judge or understand the purposes of God. Our responsibility was to obey as it says in Luke 14, Philippians 3:8, and Romans 8:28. The cost of following Christ is more than worth it. Jesus said:

> If anyone comes to Me and does not hate his father and mother and wife and children and brothers and sisters, yes, and even his own life, he cannot be My disciple. And whoever does not bear his cross and follow Me cannot be My disciple. For who

> among you, intending to build a tower, does not sit down first and count the cost to see whether he has resources to complete it? Otherwise, perhaps, after he has laid the foundation and is not able to complete it, all who see it will begin to mock him, saying, "This man began to build and was not able to complete it."
>
> —LUKE 14:26–30

Soon Vicki and I found it hard to remember why our careers had meant so much to us. God gives far better than what we can grab for ourselves. If we had stayed in those jobs and forgone His path, we would be a thousand times poorer in faith, hope, and love. And we would have missed the adventure that lay ahead.

AUSTRALIAN CONNECTION

For several months after Michael's birth I kept waking up in the middle of the night to pray for Miriam Webster, the musician from Hillsong Church in Australia who wrote "Made Me Glad" and "Exceeding Joy," the song that had helped sustain us during the pregnancy. One night the Lord told me to contact her and share some encouraging words. "Easier said than done," I told the Lord. "She's across the globe and I have no connection to her." After some diligent searching I managed to find a way to e-mail her a note. She responded that she was thankful for God's awesomeness in loving people.

I mentioned the exchange to Vicki, and the name "Miriam" prompted me to wonder aloud what the whole "Miriam Joy" thing was about.

"Miriam Webster is the only Miriam you know, so

maybe you should ask her what her middle name is," Vicki suggested.

It was a little strange asking someone I didn't know what her middle name was, but I was curious. Miriam's response electrified us: "My middle name is Joy. Why are you interested?"

Miriam Joy! I was utterly speechless. So it was a real word after all.

I told Miriam how we had been praying for "Miriam Joy" thinking it was the name of our unborn baby. Miriam wrote back that she had been going through major challenges during the months we were praying for "Miriam Joy" and that our specific prayers pertained to her situation.

"Lord, how awesome You are!" we rejoiced. "Here we were praying for Miriam Joy thinking she was our child, but those prayers were for someone we had yet to meet who was going through major struggles. You are incredible!"

Later I watched a Hillsong DVD where Miriam shared about that difficult time and how it became the inspiration for one of her new songs. Tears poured from my eyes as I considered how God had led us to pray for this woman with the earnestness of a parent for a child. "Miriam Joy" was a real word that had greatly encouraged a real person.

With that, God was about to put rocket boosters on the gift of prophecy He had given me, sending us on an amazing and sometimes overwhelming ride.

Chapter 7

HOUSE PARTY CENTRAL

NOT LONG AFTER Michael's birth, I went to work for the Staten Island financial advisor and met David Tyree. That connection, and the awesome word God gave David before the Super Bowl, was a turning point for our lives in several important ways. First, I saw that the gift of prophecy was working through me and that I should take it seriously. Second, it gave us a vision for opening our home for ministry, which led to a time of intense training in our spiritual gifts. And third, it was the first time God showed me He could open doors to well-known people without my doing anything and that He was leading me to speak to certain people at critical times in their lives.

All this was new and pretty uncomfortable to us. We would not have chosen this path, but we didn't really have a choice.

Since 2002 I had been functioning infrequently in the prophetic gifting without really knowing it. It happened almost exclusively at church or on mission trips. When led by the Spirit, I would tap someone on the shoulder, say whatever He put in my mouth to say, and then leave. I didn't think anything of it. God can use anybody to encourage others or give direction. I had never been instructed how to operate in a spiritual gift and did not characterize what I was doing as prophecy. I thought it was something everybody did.

After our experience with the church where we received the inaccurate prophecies, we eventually plugged into another church closer to home in New Jersey. One Sunday a visiting speaker prophesied from the platform, calling out people and giving them words. "Good for them," I thought. I happened to be on the worship team that day and was standing on the platform nearly hidden behind a screen. Suddenly the speaker turned and pointed to me. "Oh, no, not me!" I protested inside. In earlier days I hoped to get called out by special speakers. Now I wanted to be left alone. I was still wary of the whole idea of prophecy.

The speaker smiled, pointed at my chest, and said, "There is greatness in you." Then she went on to the next person.

"Whew! A vague word—I'm good with that," I thought and didn't pay it any more attention.

A few weeks later another guest speaker came to the church and began prophesying. He too zeroed in on me, smiled, pointed at my chest, and said, "There is greatness in you."

"The same word? What are the chances of that?" I thought, but tried to forget about it.

In the meetings that followed, Vicki received detailed prophecies about what she was going through that ministered to her greatly. I kept getting the same vague prophecy from people who had no idea who I was: "There is greatness in you." I didn't understand it, couldn't interpret it, and frankly didn't want to hear it anymore.

After our negative experience with prophecy, I decided to put the spiritual gifts to the side and not worry about them. When I received a prophetic word, I committed it to the Lord and went on with life. If it was accurate, it would unfold without my help. I refused to try to interpret it or spend energy to make it happen. Ephesians 2:10 says, "For we are His workmanship, created in Christ Jesus for good works, which God prepared beforehand, so that we should walk in them." I didn't need to figure out the plan in advance. I just needed to walk in it. That was probably the best fruit from our bad experience. We learned to not blindly accept prophetic words or stress out about them. Instead we would see if the prophecy bore witness in our spirits and lined up with the Word of God and His character. Ultimately my confidence would be in God alone, not the prophetic word.

A Prophetic Mentor

As much as I tried to keep my distance from prophecy, it kept following me. Just after meeting David Tyree, I was taken to the office of a man named Joseph Mattera. Joe was a spiritual leader in New York City, the founder and pastor of Resurrection Church in Brooklyn, and overseer of several networks of pastors and leaders in the tristate area.

The day I met Joe, a few people running for office in New York City were calling for his endorsement, and in my presence he received calls from a high-level elected official and from youth evangelist Ron Luce.

The financial advisor I worked for introduced me as he typically did: "Hubie is a CPA who works with me. If you need any help with CPA services, he can help you." Joe called me after that meeting to say he was in need of my services as a CPA because he didn't have an accountant at the time. As I began to work for him, I felt led to pray for him as I did for David Tyree, who was still recovering from a sports injury at that time. Sometimes praying for Joe kept me awake.

One day I was meeting with Joe at his office when the Lord told me to share something with him.

"Look, I have something to tell you," I said when our business meeting was finished.

"You have something to tell me?" he echoed.

"Yes. The Lord wants to tell you something," I said. My confidence had grown a little bit after sharing the word with David, though it was still frightening to obey God's leading.

"OK," Joe said.

I opened my mouth and a word came out. The whole time Joe glared at me, which was kind of scary. Then I finished speaking.

"Are you done?" he said.

"Yes."

"Let me get this straight. The Lord told you to tell me that?"

"Yeah."

"How do you know?"

"I just know," I said. "I couldn't get sleep. I got restless."

"Maybe it was something you ate," Joe said, laughing. "So how do you feel?"

"How do I feel?"

"How do you feel when it happens?" he asked.

"I don't know. I feel a stirring and it kind of happens. Why does it matter how I feel?" *Where is this conversation going?* I wondered.

"How long have you been doing this?" he pressed. Annoyed by his questions, I tried to cut it short.

"Listen, I did what I needed to do," I said. "Why are you asking me this? The word had nothing to do with me."

"No, no, no," he said. "There's a reason I'm asking. Just tell me how long."

"A few years," I answered reluctantly.

"How often does it happen?"

"I don't know. Sometimes it comes in spurts. It happens randomly."

"How accurate are you?" he asked.

"Pretty accurate," I said. "Nobody's ever looked at me crazy, and most people say it's pretty good."

I wanted to leave, so I started to excuse myself. It occurred to me that I had made a big mistake and he was closing the net on me.

"Listen, I'm going to take off," I said. "I think I'm done here."

"No, it's OK," he said. "I wanted to ask you some questions because most of the time people won't approach me."

"Approach you?"

"Yeah," he said. "You don't know much about me. People don't just give me words. Yours is very accurate. That's why I asked you those questions. You told me stuff I haven't even told my wife. You also told me stuff other people told me a long time ago."

"So it was good?"

"Yeah, it was good," he said. "You're a prophet."

"No, I'm not," I replied.

"So what do you call that?" he asked.

"I call it obeying God and getting through life like everyone else."

"You're a prophet," he repeated.

"No, I'm not. I'm just trying to hear God."

At that point, "prophecy" to me still meant something

very formal and limited. Our previous church had taught that prophecy was supposed to take place in a church. You would go to the front altar, and the pastor or prophet of the house would give you a word, then they would move on to the next person. It was your job to figure out what the word meant. The kinds of encounters I was having with people like Joe and David didn't fit that mold. They took place in everyday life, and I was not trained as a prophet. I saw what I did as encouragement, giving a message to help someone through their day or through a tough situation, but I never put two and two together and called it prophecy.

"You're a prophet," Joe said again. "I know because I am one. I have been functioning in prophetic ministry for a long time. I can look at you and know exactly what it is about you."

"OK," I said, not really knowing what that meant.

"I'm very impressed with you," he said. "You're either very courageous or very stupid."

"The way I look at it is I don't want to miss the opportunities," I said, hoping that would bring the conversation to a close.

"Who's training you and covering you?" he asked.

"I don't have anybody."

He looked at me funny.

"What about your church?" he asked.

"They don't know I do this."

"So you're just going around doing this?" he asked, incredulous. "And you've had no problem?"

"Right."

"So you don't look to do it. You just do it when God instructs you?"

"Yeah."

"How about I train you?" he asked.

"Train me?"

"Yes. I can help you since I am functioning as a prophet."

Before considering that, I thought I might turn the tables on him.

"Let me ask you something," I said. "I'm afraid to share words like I shared with you. It's scary every time. Does that ever go away?"

He looked at me intensely and with a hint of a smile. "You don't want that to go away," he said. "That keeps you in check. The fact that you're scared and don't want to but you do it anyway says a lot about your character."

"So it never goes away?" I said, losing hope for a good answer.

"You don't want it to go away."

"I guess I won't sleep any better."

He laughed. "I guess not."

A friendship began that day, and Joe indeed became my mentor in my prophetic gifting. After the Super Bowl and the David Tyree catch, Joe called me and said, "It came true! I'm so happy for you."

"Me?" I thought. "It happened to David."

"Praise God," Joe continued. "I can't wait until David starts telling everyone about you."

"Whoa, whoa," I said. "I already told him not to use my name. I don't want crazy people coming to my house. I don't want the spotlight. It's God's issue, not mine."

"You're wrong." Joe sounded emphatic.

"I'm not wrong. Scripture says to give in silence and not let your right hand know what your left hand is doing," I said.

"That's different," he said.

"No, it's about giving," I said. "I gave a word."

"That verse is about giving money, not a word," he said.

"It's the same principle," I said.

"No, it's not," he said. "You have to let David use your name."

"No, I don't," I said.

"Yes, you do," he said.

"No, I don't," I repeated.

"Go grab your Bible," he said.

He proceeded to take me through several stories: the woman at the well, prophecies given to David and Saul, and other times when prophets showed up and changed history.

"All those things happened because of prophecy," Joe said. "Now, can you imagine a story without a name on it? The prophetic messages are only validated because the prophet was mentioned. If the prophet was not mentioned, it wouldn't mean as much. You have to let David use your name because it's a modern miracle and you are short-changing what the Lord did."

"Strong words," I thought.

"I have to think about it," I said.

"You do that," he said.

"I'll pray."

"You do that," he said confidently. "When God tells you what to do, call me back."

I did pray, and the Lord began to get on my case about it. Joe was right. Six weeks after the Super Bowl I called David.

"You can use my name if you want," I conceded. Thankfully, the hype had calmed down a little and there were fewer opportunities to mention me. I told Joe he was right, and soon he was telling people what he knew about the Super Bowl story and sharing it from the pulpit.

Meanwhile, things were taking a radical turn on the home front as well.

Worship Gatherings

After the media frenzy following the Super Bowl, the Tyrees invited us to their house for some times of prayer and worship with friends and family. The gatherings were simple. At the first one about ten people showed up. Someone opened in prayer, and we began worshipping a cappella in the living room. Soon God's presence seemed to fill the room. One woman, a close friend of the Tyrees, walked in and was so overcome by the Spirit that she threw her hands in the air, fell on her knees, and started worshipping right on the spot. We all felt that way.

At some point Vicki and I were enjoying the Lord's presence when the Holy Spirit began pointing people out to me.

There. Go speak to her.

In obedience I went over to the person and shared the words the Lord put in my mouth.

There—him.

Another person caught my eye, and I walked over to him and shared a word. I was surprised at what was happening, but it seemed part of the flow of the Spirit that night. This ministry went on for a while until I felt totally drained of energy. Ministering in the Spirit is physically exhausting, and I had already worked a full day at my job. I took a break and knelt between two chairs to recover for a moment, but news had spread that the Spirit was moving and speaking to people. A woman approached Vicki, who was standing across the room from me.

"Can Hubie pray for a couple that wants to have children?" the woman asked.

The woman and her husband had just arrived, and it was the wee hours of the morning. I prayed for the woman and her husband, and the Lord told them they would indeed have a child.

We were all learning what to do when God moved, and we didn't blame people for wanting to receive ministry before the moment passed. What surprised us was their level of hunger and determination.

About a year later the woman who couldn't have children saw me at David's house and said, "Remember me?"

"No, should I?" I asked.

"I'm the woman who couldn't have children," she said. She mentioned that she and her husband came seeking a word from the Lord in the wee hours of the morning, and I began to recall the time. She said they had conceived and the baby she was holding was her child.

"Praise God!" I said.

She smiled and then turned serious and said, "You obviously hear from God, but don't pray for any more children!" With that she got up and walked away.

The Tyrees' gatherings put a new thought in our minds. If they could have worship gatherings, why not us? It seemed as simple as inviting friends over and watching God move. Perhaps this was a vision of our own future. But what a strange, unknown vision it was to us.

God then used our need for income to push us into an unforeseen "house" ministry.

I wasn't making enough as an accountant to support us, so our ears always perked at new opportunities. While I was working with a ministry, two board members were employed by Premier Jewelry, a biblically based company located in Dallas. I approached them about the possibility of us working for the company. The more we talked about it, the more it just felt like the Lord was leading us in that direction.

I couldn't help but be impressed by everyone in the company. They were such committed Christians and saw the business as a ministry to people who would never go to church. Selling jewelry in homes, when done prayerfully and with an eye toward ministry, brought opportunities to minister to customers in an informal setting. The company also made good income consistently. Women bought jewelry even in economic downturns, I learned.

Because Vicki and I had such favor with Randy and Elizabeth Draper, we felt obligated to consider this open door. God had something in it for us—we didn't know exactly what. So we took the risk and joined Premier's team as home consultants, learning how to set up displays, sell the jewelry, and network with people who might open their homes for a home show.

I liked the artsy side of it, setting up the table and displays. But because it involved jewelry, Vicki spearheaded our efforts, and the whole endeavor stretched her in many ways. Up to that point we were private people and rarely let anyone into our home. We saw our home as a fortress and retreat, not a place to socialize and entertain. Part of that was cultural and part was our personalities. Vicki grew up in New York with a grandmother who had three locks on her door and shut the blinds on the windows when she left. The idea of opening our home to friends, let alone strangers, was far from our minds.

Vicki also was discovering how uncomfortable she felt in informal social settings. At work she'd had no problem communicating, presenting, writing, and speaking to groups, but this new setting demanded different kinds of interactions. She had to learn the art of small talk, of presenting and persuading people in a home setting, of networking and making new friends. God helped her overcome a sense of awkwardness and taught her new communication skills. He also taught us to recognize ministry needs people brought, and to handle rejection and keep our hearts clean when people left without buying anything.

We never lost money selling jewelry, but God's objective was different than ours. After building new strengths into our character and prying open our front door to strangers, He brought that season to an end. Vicki became pregnant with Michael, and hosting home shows became less convenient. That brief chapter ended, but its effects were lasting.

God had given us a vision through the Tyrees for having prayer and worship gatherings, and now He had used jewelry home shows to open our home for ministry. He had spoken to us prophetically some years before that the new home we bought in New Jersey was going to be filled with people. He told us that the house would overflow with people seeking ministry and that when they showed up at the door, we would already know what to say to them. When we received that word, there was no one in our home. Naturally, when we started selling jewelry we thought, "Is this what God means? The house is not exactly overflowing, but there are people in our house and some ministry happening." As with most prophecies, we didn't know what it meant at the time and tried to interpret it by the experience we had.

One day we felt the Lord moving us to hold a worship gathering in our home and invite friends over, something we never would have considered just a year earlier. Obediently we sent out invitations via e-mail and Facebook, bought refreshments, and set up a small sound system for worship time. Four or five people showed up, and our time together was blessed. When the Lord nudged us a few months later to do it again, we were a little more eager.

Eight people showed up the next time, and Vicki and I felt that the Lord was definitely leading in this direction. Determined to let Him control every aspect of the meetings, we did not schedule one unless He moved on our hearts to do so. And we gave little structure to the gatherings. We invited people to arrive anytime after 5:30 for food and fellowship. At 7:30 or so we started worshipping. Mics and speakers were set up between the kitchen and sunken family room. Those who wanted to worship stayed in the family room or stood in the kitchen. People who wanted to relax and talk went into the living room or outside.

Against Vicki's wishes at first, I even insisted that we not plan anything about worship—how long it would go, what songs would be sung, or who would play the instruments. We simply plugged the instruments in, set up the drums, and let everything sit there until someone showed up who could play them. We knew Vicki was going to lead vocally, but we never knew who was going to show up to play for worship.

It worked much better than expected. Not once did we fail to have a player for every instrument. When one person would get tired, another would hop right in and take over. God seemed to arrange His band and treat the players interchangeably. There was little attitude or personal ambition. When someone picked up an instrument who had a wrong motivation or wasn't flowing with the Spirit, Vicki and the other players learned to overcome those situations. It was a wonderful time of discovering how to minister together, and to follow the Spirit and wait on Him until He broke through in power.

You could always sense a shift in the spiritual realm when we worshipped and the anointing fell, gently and continuously. At those moments worship would pick up to another level. It was a most beautiful, extraordinary, glorious experience in the presence of God. People would kneel with eyes closed and hands raised, receiving ministry from the Lord. When they finally got up, they actually looked different—no longer uptight and burdened but younger, glowing, and beautiful. Worship often flowed freely until after midnight.

The gatherings grew to fifty people, then one hundred people, all packed into our not-very-large house. Word got out quickly. When we invited twenty, forty showed up. When we invited forty, eighty showed up. People began e-mailing us to ask when the next one was. Some wanted it every month, but we waited for God to tell us, "Now it's time." Soon we were having them two or three times a year.

Most of the people who came were saved and hailed from different churches. Many told us that when they walked into the house, they felt something different—a freedom to worship, a closeness of the Spirit. It didn't feel any different to me, but it was clear that God was ministering in our midst. The freedom in worship was so satisfying and liberating, especially for worship leaders and others accustomed to the strict structure of a Sunday morning service. We let it flow and let the Spirit lead, and in that atmosphere He did a lot of work in the hearts of people on the verge of burnout in ministry. Nobody had to put on their church face in our home.

Plus, people had lots of fun. In summer they enjoyed the big backyard, the deck, and the pool. Some would come early and swim before worship. The gatherings became a kind of phenomenon. People wanted to be there because they knew something was happening, a special season of God moving and drawing near to those who made the effort to come.

Crash Course

On the practical side, we had some learning to do. I had experiences in catering and production due to volunteering I had done, so I knew a little about how to set up a room. The day before each gathering was a mad rush of cleaning toilets, tidying up, pushing the kitchenette and dining tables together to create a buffet, buying folding chairs, and, of course, filling a Costco cart with drinks and snacks to the tune of $1,000. If we ran short, I ordered pizza. All our clutter and extraneous decorations were dumped into boxes and temporarily put in the garage.

We naturally had concerns about hosting that many people. Would our deck collapse with the weight of too many guests? Would someone drown in the pool? Would the little kids wander away and get into mischief while their parents were worshipping? Would someone steal our valuables? Somehow those problems never materialized, and step by step we learned to trust God, prepare well, and not allow ourselves to get distracted. Even the noise we made well into the early morning hours with the windows open didn't seem to bother the neighbors in our quiet neighborhood. It was like God put a bubble of protection and favor over us.

The Tyrees came to some of the gatherings, as did actors and other high-profile people. To protect them from celebrity seekers, we made a rule that nobody could ask for autographs or take pictures with them. In those early gatherings one of the wonders was how people of all ages, cultures, and professions blended together without division. It looked like the United Nations in our house.

In that atmosphere of worship, God accelerated the use of my prophetic gift beyond what I expected. When worship got going and the anointing in the house became so thick that it felt tangible, the Holy Spirit would begin to point out individuals to me.

That one.

Him.

Her, over there.

In obedience I would go to each person and speak into his or her ear what God had given me to share. The music and conversations in the house were so loud that soon I began taking people down to the basement so they could hear what I was saying. This went on from around 8:00 p.m. to 4:00 a.m. Back and forth I would go, upstairs and downstairs. As soon as I finished with one person, the Holy Spirit would tap me on the shoulder and point out someone else. Down we would go, and I would let the Lord's words flow through me. I never knew whom He was going to point out, and I never had to prepare because God was leading the whole time. All I had to do was obey.

I quickly learned that you have to place boundaries when you minister prophetically. The first boundary is time. Some people will take as much time as you give them. Hearing from God is very personal, and in that special moment it's easy for people to forget that there are others He wants to minister to. I began using simple phrases to let people know their time was up. "Now you need to think about what He told you, ponder it, and see where God leads you," I would say to avoid a three-hour conversation. If those cues didn't work, I would tell them I needed a drink of water or to go to the bathroom. I would even cough or start fidgeting to show my discomfort. One particular woman was long-winded and wanted to know when she would meet her husband, when they would get married, and would they have any children? I had to tell her, "I'm sorry, I have no answer for you." Then I coughed and dismissed myself to get some water.

Another boundary was on the kind of information they shared. This one was harder to control. So many people had baggage they couldn't tell anyone about. Some were in leadership and were lonely at the top. When God speaks directly to your situation, it lowers your defenses and opens the floodgates. People would talk about sexual issues, affairs, substance issues, and all sorts of other things. They wanted someone to listen and care, and I sympathized with that, but ultimately that wasn't God's purpose for me. I had to find a balance of listening and caring while not becoming their counselor or "best friend" just because God had given them a word through me.

This was particularly important with women. I could see how vulnerable some women felt in those situations and how easily they could be manipulated into wrong relationships. This was the main reason I started bringing a partner with me to be present as I ministered. I established clear standards of behavior for myself. When a woman cried, I did not hug her but gave her a tissue. When a woman gave me her number and invited me to share anything else I heard from the Lord, I wouldn't call. When she went back upstairs, I would keep my distance from her the rest of the night so no personal attachment was formed. I even did this with guys so they wouldn't get the idea that I wanted to be buddies and hang out.

My comfort level in prophetic ministry began to increase dramatically. I learned to recognize the signs God used to direct me to someone. Impulses and urges that previously seemed sudden and random now felt familiar. I gained confidence in God's direction and the words that flowed. Joe was right: God wanted me to accept the gift and learn to serve in it.

I also noticed that the more I heard God and spoke His words, the more accurate and precise the words became. When ministering to hundreds of people during that season of years, you would expect something to blow up or someone to accuse you of giving them a false word. That didn't happen. Rather, people came back and verified that what God had told them had come to pass. The fruit was plentiful. People were delivered of bad habits and besetting problems. One woman's diabetes went away. Countless people were encouraged and directed by what God shared with them. People told us that attending the gathering was a once-in-a-lifetime experience for them, which is why we continued holding them as the Lord led us.

Vicki too was growing powerfully in her gift of worship. We had served in music ministry in the past, but always in a secondary role. Now Vicki was right up front. God increased her confidence in her beautiful voice and her worship-leading gift. "You can do this," He seemed to say. "Follow Me and you can."

The gatherings usually lasted two days because nobody wanted to leave. At 4:00 a.m. people would finally go home or find a couch or open spot on the floor to sleep on. Some brought sleeping bags. Out-of-town guests stayed in the kids' bedrooms and our kids doubled up. The next day we would have breakfast and worship some more until finally we had to tell people to leave.

Exhausted afterward, we would allow ourselves a week to clean up the mess in the house. Garbage had to be bagged and prioritized in the garage—how many weeks would it take to get rid of it in the weekly trash collection? Which bag would rot first? My legs felt weak and sore. My leg muscles felt like rubber bands from going up and down the stairs hour after hour. Had I known that house ministry would be so draining, I probably would have tried to avoid it. But when God tapped me on the shoulder, I could never say no. I always believed it was possibly the only time this person might receive a word, and it might be life or death for them. How could I not obey God's leading? If something bad happened, I would have been devastated. I just asked God for stamina and was thankful He didn't want us to hold the meetings every month.

After everything was cleaned up and the cost was absorbed, what stayed with us was the satisfaction of doing God's work. Our focus was relentlessly on ministry: Did we minister to enough people? Did we show them God's love and not judge them for the needs they came with? Did we feed them well and allow them to meet God right where they were?

We also learned to recognize the enemy's hand in our lives. He knew it was a powerful time and tried all kinds of ways to get under our skin. Family bickering ramped up the week before a gathering, there were misunderstandings at work, a stranger would pick a fight with one of us at the grocery store, and it seemed that Vicki and I always fell into a huge fight on the day before a gathering. We knew it was the enemy doing everything he could to sabotage God's plan. We became good at identifying his devious work and praying it out of the way.

CHASERS

We held the gatherings for five years, and in the end people actually flew in from places like Canada, Texas, Florida, and Missouri specifically to attend. Our family went from never having dinner guests to throwing open our door to whoever would come.

In the beginning we knew pretty much everyone who attended. But over time, as word got out that God was moving in worship and prophecy, we noticed a lot more strangers and a lot more people with a variety of motives. Some wanted to spy out the celebrities and athletes. Others wanted to network with other Christians. Some wanted to be where the action was, some were curious, and some were truly desperate for an answer. We knew people came with different intentions and we couldn't control that. Our commitment was to keep the door open and create an atmosphere of worship so that everyone would feel a touch from God.

Even so, at times our home was full of people we had never seen before, and that was kind of scary.

Perhaps predictably, the gatherings began to attract prophecy chasers. These people, almost always strangers, didn't want to relax and spend time worshipping and getting to know other people. They came with one purpose: to have me minister to them. "Where's the basement?" they would ask, knowing that I ministered to people there. Some tried to cut in line if I had several people waiting.

"I drove from Long Island and have to go," one woman told me. "Do you think you can pray for me first?"

Another woman we didn't know brought a cake and was determined to get downstairs before everyone else. Some interrupted me as soon as I came upstairs, and I had to tell them, "I'm in the middle of something. You have to wait." Others openly asked, "Who is this guy? How accurate is he? How do I get downstairs?" The gatherings became more about seeing me than seeking God, which was the original goal. That really bothered us.

To make it worse, David put my name in his book without my knowledge. That added to the number of people dropping by to "get a word." One time I went to David's book signing and a guy came up to me and just stood there. David said to the man, "This is Hubie."

The man replied, "I know who he is. Listen, you got anything to say to me?"

I didn't, and I never felt pressured to perform for people. If God didn't give me anything to say, I had no problem telling them, "Read your Bible if you want a word." Some people were more subtle about it and wanted to insinuate themselves into our personal lives. We had to tell them gently that we didn't have time to be friends with everyone.

Part of me remained perplexed by the fuss people made over this particular gift, and I began to have an identity problem. People were no longer coming just to worship and seek God, to deepen friendships with us and others. It seemed that more and more people didn't care about Hubie and Vicki but about the things we had to offer them—prophecy and an atmosphere of worship. I began to feel like every time someone wanted a word, they were rejecting me as a person. Hard feelings emerged toward people I should have loved and served, and I even felt depressed after some gatherings.

David Tyree ministered to me out of his own experience. He had dealt with the fame chasers, the people wanting his autograph while not caring about him as a person. He helped me see it differently—that God was indeed working through me and the opportunities to minister even when people had mixed motives. God cared about me even when people didn't seem to, and He still wanted to give them answers and direction, even if their intentions were not pure. That advice was critical to help me maintain a clean heart toward God and people. I was grateful for David's timely and godly wisdom.

Soon the Holy Spirit told us we were done holding worship gatherings at our home—He was bringing that season to a close and moving us to another one. I never would have guessed it involved ministering to well-known musicians through one of my favorite hobbies.

Chapter 8

VOICING AMPS FOR THE ROCK STARS

Music was a huge part of my life from my earliest years. My mom would put on "The Lion Sleeps Tonight" by The Tokens or "The Twist" by Chubby Checker. She, my sister, and I would dance by the record player for what seemed like hours. Mom couldn't sing, and I inherited that trait, but we did our best. I loved music so much that I left my radio on all day and all night, even when I slept. When I woke up, I would lie in bed until a good song came on to get me going. I played a lot of air guitar, and some real guitar, and dreamed of being a big rock star one day.

As an adult, I reacquainted myself with the guitar and found I was just as talented as when I had put it down as a kid—that is, not really talented at all. But I had passion that far outpaced my skills and I doggedly stuck with it, giving myself lessons even when my fingers turned purple. What I didn't know was that God planned to use my hobby and a technical skill I picked up almost by accident from one of the world's great amplifier makers to put me in the path of well-known musicians who needed to hear from God.

TRAINWRECK

One of my accounting clients, a guy in Chicago, was into buying and selling vintage guitars, and we talked about the subject of vintage tone now and then. He recommended I change the pickups in my guitar to get a better tone and introduced me to a guy I'll call Bill, who made really good pickups. (Pickups are the electronic parts that sit under the guitar's strings and pick up the sound.) Bill and I struck up a friendship, and one day I mentioned that I was looking for a better amplifier. "I have a friend who can make you one," Bill said. "Call this number. It'll be the amp of your dreams." I obeyed blindly and called, not knowing who was on the other end. The message machine picked up: "Hi, you have reached Ken Fischer."

I almost dropped the phone. Ken Fischer was a living legend in the world of guitar amplifiers. Since the 1980s he had hand-made amps and modified amps for leading rock guitarists, including Eddie Van Halen, Mark Knopfler, Richie Sambora, and bands such as ZZ Top and Metallica. Nobody could make amps sound the way Ken did. He was a true artisan and a brilliant eccentric. He called his amps Trainwrecks and made them out of his home in New Jersey. They currently cost $40,000 or more.

I was so surprised to realize who I had called that I started to hang up without leaving a message. Then I heard a voice. "Hello?"

By-passing the big lump in my throat, I forced out, "Hi."

"Hi," the man said.

"My name is Hubie," I said lamely.

"Nice to meet you."

"Bill told me to call you."

That warmed him up. "Oh, Bill is one of my best friends. What can I do for you?"

"I'm looking for an amp," I said, disbelieving that this conversation was actually taking place.

Ken said he had licensed the amp building to Komet Amplifiers in Baton Rouge, but he still built a few amps. "If you want one, you'll have to wait about a year," he said. "I don't feel well all the time and I won't give it to you unless it sounds good. I'm finishing up a couple of amps now for Richie Sambora of Bon Jovi so they can use them for a video they are shooting in a few days." The video was for the song "Have a Nice Day."

"OK, I'll wait," I said.

"Don't send me any money," he said. "I'll put you on the list. How good of a player are you? What kind of music do you play?"

"Worship music."

"So you play rhythm. You want it to sound pretty."

"I guess so," I said.

"OK. Give me about a year. I will call you when your name is coming up on the list," he said, and after a few more details we hung up. I called Bill right away.

"What are you doing, giving me Ken Fischer's number?" I said.

Bill laughed hysterically. "I told you it'd be the amp of your dreams," he said.

Ken called a couple of months later. "I'm working on your amp," he said. "Someone canceled, and since you're a friend of Bill's, I'm doing yours next. What kind of tubes do you want?"

I didn't even know what tubes were. He explained that the best electric guitar amps make their sound by sending electricity through a series of glass tubes. The tubes resist and absorb the flowing energy to varying degrees, creating an electric guitar sound.

"Here's a list of tubes to look for from the fifties and sixties," he said. "They sound better than the Chinese and Russian tubes you can get today."

The right tubes would give my amp richer, mellower sounds than modern tubes, he promised. I started hunting online for old tubes and saw that they sold for $200 or $300 each. "What's Vicki going to think of all this?" I thought as I pondered the potential cost of an amp of this caliber. But something made me want to spend the money. "If I'm going to get an amp from Ken Fischer, I might as well do it right," I thought.

I bought some old tubes, and Ken told me to swing by his house to drop them off because he happened to live fairly close. I found his place and knocked on the door with $1,000 worth of tubes in a box, intending to leave them on the porch as he had instructed me. I started to walk away when his mother answered the door. "Would you like to come in?" she asked. Just then, Ken came up from his shop. He seemed annoyed that I was invading his space. I knew Ken suffered from a chronic illness and that he rarely left his house and did not let many people see him in person.

"You're here," he said grumpily. "You might as well come see the shop."

Down we went to his basement, and I found myself in the heart of the beast. This humble room, paneled in wood and littered with wires, electronic equipment, and tools, was where Ken practiced his genius. I sat down, and we shot the breeze about guitar sounds on certain songs we knew, and the merits of certain guitars and pickups. He talked about how bands from the sixties and seventies each had unique guitar sounds because the amps and components they used were unique. You could tell who the band was just by listening to the guitar. Nowadays every guitarist sounds the same because amps are mass produced and do not use vintage tubes.

It was a nice conversation, and the connection I felt with Ken surprised me.

"I'll call you when I have something," he said as I headed out.

After our introduction, Ken stayed on my mind. I kept thinking about the illness that made him depressed and reclusive. One day I went to a health food store and got him some alternative medicine for his stomach, dropped it off on his porch, and called him later to let him know it was there.

"I put something on your porch for you," I said.

"Why'd you do that?" he asked.

"To help you," I said.

He expressed cautious appreciation but seemed a little suspicious.

I kept praying about Ken's situation and soon felt a nudge to buy him something bigger—a MacBook. Ken didn't know how to use computers but had told me he was thinking of finally taking the plunge since his friends were urging him to buy one. With Vicki's approval I had the laptop delivered to his house and soon got a call from him.

"What'd you do that for?" Ken asked harshly. "What do you want?"

"You said you wanted a computer," I said.

"I'm not going to give you a discount on your amp," he said.

"I don't want a discount. You said you wanted one, so I got you one. No strings attached."

It took him a bit to understand that I wasn't trying to get anything in return. At first he refused to use the computer because he would not use any electronic device until he had taken it apart to see how it worked. Eventually he used the MacBook to watch movies.

Around that time he began calling me regularly. We both worked from home and had the luxury of chatting while we worked. I would put him on speakerphone and we would shoot the breeze for hours. Ken loved to talk and had a mind like an encyclopedia. Mixed in with the mundane details of his day, he would share how Jimi Hendrix got certain sounds from his guitar, and about the work Ken had done with Joe Perry of Aerosmith, Mark Knopfler, and Kirk Hammett, the guitarist from Metallica. Sometimes he would turn on his stereo and play something for me by an artist who was using one of his amps.

Soon Ken was being generous in return. He bought scientific puzzles and a crystal radio set for my kids. I found myself at his house now and then, hanging out while he worked. Ken loved to teach while building his amps. He knew all the science behind the sound, and I began to learn from him. He showed me how to make an amp sound better by installing the right tubes. Cheap modern tubes make guitars sound bright and brittle on high notes, but old vintage tubes absorb a lot more energy for a mellower tone that doesn't pierce your eardrums. The sound comes from electrons flowing through the wires and meeting resistance in the tubes. Distortion takes place when electrons flood the tubes to overload. I was amazed at everything that went into it and how much Ken knew. His gift for "voicing" amps was unlike anything I had ever seen or heard of.

One day several amps arrived in boxes from Komet

Amplifiers while I was there. I carried them downstairs for him. He put his hands on the first box, and without even plugging it in he said, "This one's not good. I have to send it back." When we plugged it in, sure enough, it did not meet his sound quality. When he put his hands on the other box he said, "Now this is a good one." We plugged it in, and it sounded fantastic. I'm still not sure how he knew just by touching the box.

Ken showed me how the order of tubes in their slots mattered as well. Some vintage Marshall amps have three preamp tubes. Vox amps have many more, and so do Fenders. When you change the order of the tubes in their slots, it changes the sound significantly depending on the individual tube. Like a kid with a science kit, Ken would experiment by trying all combinations of tube types and sequences until he hit on a sound he liked. Even tubes from the same manufacturer in the same shipment could sound different. He taught me that everything is open to experimentation and that you pull the best out of an amp by exploring all the possibilities.

Tubes were just the beginning. Ken believed that every single component of an amplifier and guitar affects the sound. The quarter-inch cord connecting the head to the cabinet mattered, as did the cord from the amp to the guitar. Even little things you would never think of fell under his scrutiny. He showed me how to improve the sound by tightening or loosening the screws on the guitar's pickups and pick guard, and the screws on the amp itself. He told me which guitar strings to use. One time he unscrewed an amp from its cabinet to demonstrate how different it sounds when it is outside the cabinet.

Ken could even "bias," or "tune," an amp by plugging in a guitar and listening to the white noise alone, without strumming the guitar. His dog ears could hear things I couldn't hear even after he pointed them out. It started to make sense to me why guitarists could feel the difference when playing through a Trainwreck or anything else Ken touched. Ken let no detail go unnoticed, and the resulting sound was amazing.

One day Ken called me. "Go on eBay and look for the most beat-up old vacuum cleaner you can find," he said. "Buy it and then tell them to clip the cord and send it to you. You don't want the whole thing. Tell them it is for a science experiment."

"What's this for?" I asked.

"You're going to make a wire from the head to the cabinet," he said.

When the vacuum cleaner power cords arrived, Ken had me solder the ends to plugs and plug them into the amp and cabinet. The quality of the sound changed dramatically! Then he had me switch the ends of the cable, and the sound changed again. Even which end goes in made a difference! Everything mattered.

Ken's spiritual ideas were looser and more free-form. He believed in "the universe" and various things picked up from Native American and Eastern religions. In essence, he believed in anything. But I believe God was in our relationship somehow. I well remember the day Ken called and said, "Next time you come over, bring your guitar. I'm working on this Trainwreck and want you to hear it." I took my guitar over and played it through the Trainwreck amp. Ken leaned back, closed his eyes, and listened to the rich, beautiful sound coming from his handmade work of art. I could feel the presence of God in that room, deep, powerful, and yearning. After a while Ken opened his eyes.

"Magic," he said. I knew better.

Our conversations about God never seemed to go anywhere, and I wondered sometimes what the purpose of our relationship was, aside from my enjoying Ken and his work. He named the amp he made for me "Gracie," after a nickname for my daughter Sara. Ken's amps didn't have serial numbers; rather, he named them after women. "Every amp is different," he would say. "Every female is different. They're never the same."

Three years after I met him, Ken succumbed to his chronic illness and passed away just before Christmas. It was a devastating loss. I had purchased an amp he really wanted and was going to give it to him a few days later. Sadly, it was too late. A close friend was gone, and the music industry lost a true original. His handmade amps—fewer than a hundred of them in existence—are still coveted by top musicians.

Carrying the Legacy

I didn't know it, but my experience with Ken had a continuing purpose. For several years I had taken tons of mental notes on what Ken taught me. It was essentially a master's course in voicing amps, a specialized skill and a dying art. The information seemed somewhat pointless to me after Ken died.

Then Vicki and I went to a Switchfoot concert at a two-day rock festival called Revolution Generation, or RevGen. We were there to see another band but stayed for Switchfoot. Standing near the stage, I could see Switchfoot's guitarist playing through a vintage amp. All the other bands were using recently manufactured amps, so his old-school one stood out to me. I also noticed him switching guitars, which I found interesting.

The concert was really good. When we came home, the Lord impressed on me, "You need to contact him," meaning the guitarist. I asked my daughter who he was and poked around on the Internet for an e-mail address. All I could find was his management company, so I sent a note that said, "I noticed you have a vintage amp. I can probably make it sound better." About a month later the guitarist, Drew Shirley, replied to my e-mail, which he later told me was unusual because he usually didn't reply to e-mails from people he did not know. We started talking about guitars and tone, and I passed on what I learned from Ken about refining a guitar amp's sound. Drew started experimenting with Ken's advice and one day sent me a lengthy e-mail. "My life has totally changed," he said, referring to the new tone he had achieved. "I cannot believe what this sounds like." It had taken his creativity to a whole new level, he said.

When Switchfoot came to town again, they gave my family backstage passes, and we hung out before and after the show. Drew told us how the band had won a lot of Dove Awards, which was a great honor but didn't give them much credibility in the secular world. Their dream was to win a Grammy. Right as we were saying good-bye, the Lord stirred me, and I gave Drew a word. The only thing I remember about it was, "You are going to win a Grammy."

Switchfoot self-produced an album called *Hello Hurricane*. The album was doing OK on the charts, then out of the blue it was nominated for a Grammy for Best Rock or Rap Gospel Album. At the Grammy ceremony Drew used his iPhone to record the moment when the envelope was opened—and Switchfoot won! He sent me the video afterward as a souvenir. It felt like we were there celebrating with them. It was truly a special moment for me because they are awesome guys, and I was humbled by the fact that the Lord used me to encourage them. It is quite an experience to be used by the Lord to share something with someone and then see what was prophesied actually happen!

God began opening other doors to talk to Christian musicians about their guitar and amp tones. The irony of it never escaped me. Here I was, a musically non-talented, tone-deaf accountant from New Jersey having in-depth conversations with professional musicians about making their music sound better. Talk about using the foolish things of the world! That was me all over. God had given me specialized knowledge that opened doors to guys who needed help with their music—and needed to hear things from the Lord.

One of those doors was to a very well-known country music singer whose name I will not share. I was watching the Country Music Awards one night and saw this particular performer playing through a Trainwreck amp. He had bought it after Ken died, and for some reason the amp didn't sound its best to my ears. A friend suggested I get in touch with the singer through Twitter to discuss improving the amplifier's tone. So one day when this famous singer tweeted "My amp sounds so great," I replied that I could make it sound better.

This guy has millions of followers, but he followed me and direct messaged me his e-mail address. I sent some suggestions and never heard back. After a while I left him with, "If you want to hear from me, e-mail me back. Otherwise I'll leave you alone." I didn't want him to feel like I was chasing him. I wanted to help if he wanted it. I was stunned to get a reply from him saying, "I'm sorry! Been busy. Let's get together when I'm in town."

This singer came to our area for a show and invited me

to the arena beforehand. I took some vintage tubes with me, ready to experiment if necessary. I was directed to park in the back of the arena, and a driver picked me up in a golf cart. "Lord, what is going on?" I thought as he whisked us into the bowels of the building. The country music star was doing a sound check and walked over to introduce himself to me. He shook my hand and said, "There she is," pointing to the Trainwreck amp sitting nearby like a faithful friend.

"Go ahead and make it sound better," he said with a smile.

Peering into the back of the familiar cabinet, I saw that he had good, vintage tubes, but they were out of order. Ken had taught me to put them in a certain order, which improves the bass tones and clarity of the notes. In just a few seconds I switched the order of the tubes and invited the singer to play through the amp again. He started ripping out licks. His guitar technician nodded. The singer smiled. The tone sounded significantly better.

"Wow," the singer said, playing some more. "Man, that didn't take long." He and his guitar technician looked at each other like, "What did this guy do?" I showed him what I had done with the tubes and explained why it mattered. He was enjoying the new tone so much that he wouldn't stop playing. "This is going on the record," he said. Before I left I voiced a few of his amps, and he said he would keep in touch.

The change in guitar tone was apparent on the next album he released. When he was in concert in New Jersey again, I went to the show. As we spoke before the concert, he suggested that one day I should go to Nashville to see his studio and work on some of his other amps. It didn't feel right, and I was busy with work deadlines, so I thought I might go one day in the future.

When the singer came to town again for another concert, he invited my family backstage, and there God opened more doors for ministry. After the show the Lord directed me to minister to a singer who had opened for him. It turns out he was a Christian, and his whole family was there with him. The Lord gave words to him and each of his family members in his dressing room.

I left thinking, as I usually did, "How on earth does this stuff happen?"

Rhythm Section

I had grown in confidence in my gift because of the intensive training God put us through in our house ministry. It was easier for me to recognize when He wanted me to share a word with someone, and I was usually quicker to obey, though it still scared me. Doors for ministry kept opening.

One day a friend named Storm asked to me to go a Sheila E concert with him. I had met Storm through our church. He was a muscular state trooper with an air of authority about him. He hosted a men's fellowship at his house, and I was amazed to find the place packed with guys who were excited to worship, pray, and dive into the Word. Seldom had I seen so many men eager to talk about Jesus. It was a very cool event, and Storm and I got to know each other.

At one point I shared a word from the Lord with Storm involving the restoration of a broken relationship in his wife's life. The restoration seemed impossible at the time, but in a few months it happened just as the Lord had said. Storm became very interested in how God worked supernaturally and invited me to breakfast to explore the subject more. I thought we would chat casually, but he brought his notepad and pencil and plied me for stories about how the spiritual gifts worked. He was eager to learn, and I was happy to share what little I knew.

One day Storm became convinced that we should attend a Sheila E concert and see what God would do. He was a big fan of hers and tried to convince me to go. I was skeptical. I knew only a couple of her songs, and it wasn't my type of music. Still, I had a feeling God had some business for me at the concert.

"OK, Lord," I said after breakfast with Storm. "If You want me to go, I'll go. But I don't want to drive. And I don't want to have to work tomorrow."

Within hours Storm called and offered to drive, and my appointments for the next day got postponed. My conditions had been met, and I couldn't say no anymore. Storm was giddy when I accepted. "Something's going to happen tonight," he said.

"I don't know if anything will happen," I kept telling him. "It's not up to me." But he rubbed his hands together with glee.

We got to the venue at Times Square, and the crowd was standing room only. People were buying tickets and moving to the side to stand against the wall. We bought tickets, and a woman looked at us and said, "Come with me." We didn't know who she was, but we followed her as she led us to a table near the stage on the dressing room side.

"See?" Storm said, smiling. "I know something's going to happen."

We ordered dinner and listened to the opening band play rhythm and blues. Then Sheila E came out and put on a very good show. When she finished her encore, Storm looked at me, his eyes brightening. "Now the good stuff," he said.

"Do you really want to stay after?" I asked, wishing we could just go home. But I knew better. The Lord had made it clear to me in the meantime that I had an assignment there.

We got in line with the fans waiting for autographs and photos with Sheila E. While waiting, I asked the Lord specifically what I should do. As usual, He didn't tell me anything except that He had something to share with her. I was reluctant. The setup was different than how it usually happened. I never "chased" people to give them words but let God open doors all the way. It didn't strike me as appropriate to ambush someone with a word, but my desire to be obedient outweighed my desire for comfort.

Our turn came, and I tried to be brief. Storm looked on with intense curiosity.

"I liked your show," I said to Sheila. "Can I pray for you?"

"No, I'm good," she said, and I didn't blame her. I was a complete stranger. But I knew I had an assignment.

"You sure?" I asked.

"No, I'm good," she said, nodding her head vigorously.

"The Lord wants to tell you a couple of things," I said.

"No, I'm good," she repeated.

"See?" I said to the Lord.

I respected her words and walked away not realizing that Storm had stayed behind. Unbeknownst to me he had pulled out his badge to show Sheila we had credibility and weren't just crazy celebrity-seekers.

I turned around to see Storm coming.

"You said hi to her?" I said.

"I kind of whipped out my badge," he said.

"You did what?"

"You have stuff to say to her," he said. "This is serious. I figured I'd do my part."

"You didn't need to do that," I said. "God works it out."

Just then a big guy came after us.

"I'm Sheila's manager," he said. "Come over to the table. She wanted me to ask you what you want to tell her."

I hesitated.

"I do have something to share with her," I said, "but I don't really want to tell it to other people."

"It's OK," he assured me. "She said to have you tell me and I'll tell her. She has a line of people out front and a line backstage, so it's going to be awhile. She and I are really close friends. She's the godmother of my children."

"OK," I said after a moment of consideration. We sat down and the word came forth. As the manager listened, he began nodding his head, then shaking his head almost in disbelief. When I finished, he said, "You don't know her—but you do know her."

As usual, I had nothing else to say. My assignment was over.

"OK," I said. "That's what it is."

"I'll be sure to tell her," he said. "Can I get your e-mail?"

I gave it to him, and my Twitter name. As we started to leave, I felt another nudge.

"By the way," I said, turning to the manager, "God wants to bless you because you were faithful in chasing me down."

He sat back down and out came another word telling him how his career had gone, where it was now, and where it was going in the future. God didn't want him to be afraid of what was to come. Then God started giving me words about his kids, their gifts, and what their lives were supposed to be like. The manager looked at Storm and me in complete amazement.

"You don't even know me," he said. "There's no way you could have known about my children. I'll get ahold of you."

"OK," I said, and we shook hands and parted.

On the way out Storm was gleeful. "See, I knew something was going to happen," he said. "Any more people in the crowd you want to talk to?"

"No," I said. "Let's get out of here."

The next day I woke up and saw a Twitter notification that Sheila E was now following me. "I guess the manager delivered the message," I thought. The Lord had me share a couple more words via Twitter direct message in subsequent months, and she replied graciously, "Come and see me in concert!" And then, "How do you know this stuff?"

I was watching God use my hobby to create pathways to share messages with people of all kinds in the most unexpected ways. I learned that He is interested in everything we do and wants to use all our interests in creative ways for His glory. Even the most unlikely things in our lives can open doors supernaturally. That's why obedience without understanding is so important in any of the gifts. He knows a lot better than we do.

Just ahead was an encounter not with a rock star but with a minister who was known locally but whose book would soon take America by storm.

Chapter 9

THE HARBINGER

I WAS COMING HOME from Florida on a ministry trip when the Lord gave me my first assignment to a stranger in an airport.

As is too often the case, I was not in the best of moods when I dragged myself to the self-serve check-in kiosk at the airport. Florida had been a whirlwind, and I had stayed longer than planned because doors for ministry had expanded. Now I was ready to go home and collapse. I put my credit card in the check-in kiosk and prepared to select my seat—always on the aisle because I like to drink lots of water on flights.

But something happened that has never happened to me before or since: without giving me any options, the machine spit out my tickets with my seats already selected. It had given me a window seat on my second flight. "Great," I thought. For the second leg of the journey I would be dehydrated the whole time, or else climbing over fellow passengers constantly to get to the restroom. My mood sagged more.

I missed my wife and kids, was concerned with the amount of work to do once I got home, and was feeling sad because Ken Fischer had just died and I had missed the funeral due to this trip. I got off the plane in Charlotte and was ready to cheer myself up with some Dickey's barbecue. Food in hand, I found a seat in the gate area and was just digging in when the Lord started nudging me. "You've got to talk to that guy."

As usual, details were scarce, and I thought maybe fatigue was working on me. Plus, I was really hungry and didn't feel like ministering to anybody. I ignored the nudge and kept eating. When the Lord nudged me again, I pointed out with some annoyance that nobody was sitting nearby.

"Look up," He said.

Twenty feet away was a guy on a cell phone having what appeared to be an intense conversation.

"Him."

"Lord—no. I'm going to eat. I'm tired and hungry. I ministered in Florida the whole time I was there. I need a break."

The barbecue was delicious, but my stomach began turning. Now I was genuinely upset.

"I really can't believe You're going to make me do this," I thought. The food was so good, but my stomach was working against me. It's no use trying to eat when your stomach hurts. I gave up. "OK, Lord, just let me finish this barbecue. Then I'll wash my hands and talk to this guy before I get on the plane."

I ate quickly, adjourned to the restroom to wash up, and came back. The guy was still on his cell phone. I had never approached someone I didn't know in an airport, so I did the only thing I could think of: I walked over, stood in front of him, and stared. He noticed me and looked down. When he looked back up I was still there, staring at him.

"Hold on a minute," he told his caller, then said to me with a deep Southern accent, "Yeah, whatchu want?"

"The Lord wants me to tell you a couple things," I replied.

"Yeah?"

"Yeah."

At that moment the word from the Lord started coming out as if a faucet had been turned on. It went for maybe ten seconds, but it seemed like an eternity. I kept wondering what the guy on the other end of the line was thinking. Before I could finish, the man held up his hand, put the phone back to his ear, and said, "I gotta call you back." He hung up. "OK, now continue." The word flowed again, and he listened without any discernible expression. It appeared he might be staring me down, but I couldn't let that concern me. His reaction wasn't my business. I was just there to deliver the message.

After it was done, I said, "You got it?" I felt unburdened and was ready to disappear and continue with my day, wishing I had waited to enjoy the barbecue at a more leisurely pace.

"Yeah," he said.

"I gotta catch my flight," I said, dismissing myself.

"You mean this flight right here?" he said in his big, helpful Southern accent.

"Yes," I said.

"I'm on that flight too!" he said. "Where are you sitting?"

I pulled out my ticket, the one the machine had spit out without giving me a choice of seats.

"Look at that!" he said. "We're sitting right next to each other."

Minutes later I found myself on the plane with this man, his wife, and another couple they were with. The man I had spoken with, Dick Barber, must have told them what had happened because they were looking at me expectantly.

"So, do you do this often?" Dick asked. "We've never had anything like that happen before. What you said was really accurate."

"That's a relief," I thought.

Intrigued by what had happened, they asked about my ministry of accosting strangers in airports with supernatural information. I told them it was the first time this had happened in an airport, and then I got to hear their side of the story. Dick was an elder at a church in North Carolina and was traveling with his wife, Jane, and another couple. The Barbers had just been through a church split and were left holding the bag after everyone left. The Lord's word to them had been essentially, "Don't worry. It's going to grow. Stay where you need to be."

"What the Lord told you to say really hit home with us on where we are and where we are going, personally and as a church," Dick said. They were heading on vacation, and the Lord had relieved their hearts of needless anxiety so they could enjoy themselves.

"So, can you talk to this one?" Dick asked, pointing to the other man traveling with him.

The Lord indeed gave words to each of them, and when we landed, we prayed together and went our different ways. They kept in touch by e-mail, and I heard about how their church began growing and flourishing again. Dick also mentioned that all four of them had been sick in various ways and to varying degrees before we met. He later told me that after we prayed at the Newark airport, they all were immediately better and had a great trip because of the healings.

Dick called our encounter his "touched by an angel"

experience, which I love because when the Lord shares information with you, it makes you feel special. He is such a good God. The part we play in these situations is so small. What God did was as marvelous to me as it was to Dick and his group.

Jonathan Cahn in the Charlotte Airport

Perhaps the Lord orchestrated the encounter with Dick to prepare me for the encounter with Jonathan Cahn a couple of years later. Or maybe the Lord just likes doing surprising things in the Charlotte airport. In any case, the day I met Jonathan could not have been worse for me on so many levels. My older sister had been diagnosed with stomach cancer and had little time to live, according to doctors. She and I had been estranged for years, and my visiting her was freighted with a great deal of tension. We had not spoken for so long. Now it was time to sort things out, mend what we could, mourn what had been lost, and perhaps salvage some resolution from a relationship the enemy had wrecked.

My stress level was higher than usual because the visit was taking place during my second busiest season of the year, which falls in October. That's when six-month tax extensions come due, on October 15, and all sorts of paperwork must be submitted to the IRS. On top of that, a Nor'easter came crashing into the coast, canceling a bunch of flights and threatening my itinerary. The rain was whipping and the airline kept sending me voice mails: "Your flight has been delayed... Your flight has been delayed." Every hour the phone rang with that familiar message, and finally I called to talk with a real person. With my flight now leaving at 10:00 p.m., and no connection to

Dallas until the next morning, I had them book me on the earliest flight the next day. It was a lot better than sleeping in the terminal or an airport hotel in Charlotte.

I stayed up all night working on tax returns because I had to be at the Newark airport at 3:00 a.m. for a 5:00 a.m. flight, which meant leaving the house at 2:30 a.m. for the airport. It rained all night, a dismal sound track to the sea of numbers in which I was immersed. When I got to the airport, even the ticket counters were closed. Passengers like me wandered around dazed, faces pale under the energy-saving lights, each of us wishing for a warm bed. At some point in that zombielike state I remember catching a glimpse of an Orthodox Jewish man among those marking time. I paid him no mind.

I couldn't sleep on the flight from Newark to Charlotte, and when we landed, I got the largest coffee on the menu and found a seat to slouch in, which wasn't easy with all the people waiting at the airport due to flight delays because of the weather. Rock music filled my ears and thoughts of lost time with my sister filled my mind.

"I've already missed Friday because of the rainstorm," I thought. "I even lost a lot of productivity with work because I was standing by for a flight. Now I'll get to Dallas and have a short time before turning around and heading home. What a bunch of wasted time."

The music carried my mind away for a moment, and then suddenly the Lord spoke to my heart. "You've got to speak to the guy."

I responded almost immediately, "I'm not speaking to anybody. I am in no mood to do anything!"

Tired, thoroughly annoyed, slouching there like a teenager in my hoodie, jeans, and sneakers, I turned my iPod louder and sipped my coffee, willing away the persistence of the Holy Spirit. But then my stomach started to turn.

"No," I said. "I'm not going to do it. I don't feel well. Don't You know how I feel?"

My stomach kept churning, and I was really starting to feel sick. God does not give up easily. So I glanced over and saw a man dressed in black—the Orthodox Jewish man I had noticed earlier.

"Lord, I've got nothing to say to this guy. He's Jewish. He's still waiting for the Messiah. I know You came already."

I kept sipping my coffee.

"Plus, I don't want to look like an idiot," I concluded.

Nudge.

I looked over nonchalantly again and saw that the man was reading a little book. "Wonder what that is," I thought and leaned back so I could see it out of the corner of my eye. It was the Bible's Book of Proverbs.

"See, Lord? I'm off the hook. It's Old Testament. I'm not going to do this."

Back to my coffee, back to my iPod. But the feeling in my stomach only got worse. I thought I might actually get sick right there in the terminal. I glanced over again. Now the man was slouching in his seat, hands near his shoulders, palms outspread in what appeared to be a posture of praise. He was bobbing the way I've seen Orthodox Jewish people do when they pray.

"This guy is clearly Orthodox. I have nothing to say. I must be hearing You wrong. Maybe it's the lack of sleep."

The Lord's prompting was strong: "*You need to speak to him.*"

On the verge of throwing up, I relented, took out my

earbuds, put my right arm on the broken seat between us, and said, "What's the good word?"

"God loves you," the man said almost without hesitation.

"God loves me. All right, Lord, You're doing something here," I thought. As we chit-chatted, I waited on the Lord for guidance.

"What do you do?" he asked.

"Accountant. You?"

"Speaker. Where are you going?"

"Dallas," I said.

"Me too."

"What kind of speaker are you?"

"I'm on the radio. My show is called *Two Nice Jewish Boys*."

"Oh, I used to listen to you."

"Used to?" he said. "What happened?"

We both laughed.

"I'm in a type of ministry as well," I said.

"What kind of ministry?"

"I usually minister to people backstage, giving encouragement," I said.

An announcement came over the PA that our flight was boarding.

"It's been good talking to you," he said and began to stand.

"You too," I said.

"*Now,*" the Lord said, virtually hitting me over the head. I sighed and got ready for the potentially awkward moment.

"You can't get up yet," I said.

"Oh?" he replied. He sat back down cautiously.

"The Lord wants to tell you a few things."

Suddenly the word started flowing from my mouth.

The man stared at me with no emotion, the way a person looks at a crazy man. As usual, I didn't know what I was saying. When it finished, we looked at each other like, "What now?" His expression gave me no hint of what he was thinking.

"You got it?" I said. I often ask people that just to make sure it sticks in their heads and they really consider the words, because I sure can't e-mail it to them later.

He replied, "Are you on this flight?"

"Yes."

"When we go up, I'm going to come find you. You're going to share all of that with me again."

"I can't."

"You have to."

"It doesn't work that way. I've never done that."

"No, this is a life-and-death thing. It's for the country," he said with more confidence than I felt. He got in line to board, and when the plane reached cruising altitude, I found myself at the back of the airplane with him. Prayer indeed released the word again, and it came out in even greater detail than before. The man, Jonathan Cahn, wrote page after page of notes. Then he began asking me questions.

"How does this happen? How do you feel?"

I told him I didn't feel anything and that my mind went blank as the word passed through me.

"That is like prophets in the Bible," he said, "Jonah, Daniel. That's how they felt. Have you done this for others?"

"Yes," I said and mentioned David Tyree. After a little more conversation we returned to our seats, and I was relieved to be alone again. "I delivered my thing, Lord. Now it's time to relax."

When we landed in Dallas, Jonathan was waiting for me outside the plane.

"You're going to baggage claim, right?" he said.

"Yes."

We started walking toward the baggage claim.

"I want to do something for you," Jonathan said. "I want to pray for you. I want to give you the Aaronic blessing."

At baggage claim we found a corner that was only slightly hidden from sight, and he started saying a prayer over me in Hebrew. "Is this really happening?" I thought, trying to receive it but feeling conspicuous. I spied my brother-in-law who was there to pick me up. He saw the Jewish man praying over me and was clearly confused. I held up my hand to indicate for him to wait. When Jonathan finished blessing me, we shook hands, and he left. My brother-in-law approached cautiously. "What was that all about?" he asked.

"Just a guy I met on the plane," I said. "Don't worry about it."

SUPERNATURAL PUBLICATION

I didn't think much about the encounter. Jonathan had told me little about his situation, and I didn't care to know any more. I remember him saying that God had given him a book, and he was flying to Dallas to see a literary agent but wasn't feeling right about it. Jonathan said he had been praying in the Charlotte airport that God would have His way at the meeting with the agent when I struck up conversation.

We kept loosely in touch over the next few months. Jonathan remembered that I had met Charisma House publisher Steve Strang through David Tyree's book and that I had mentioned I could possibly reach out to him regarding his book. Sometime after that Jonathan asked me if I would contact Steve about his manuscript. I was reluctant because my relationship with Steve was fairly new. The last thing I wanted was to disrupt the Lord's work. Since I had never asked for anything, I did not want to change our relationship. I didn't even know what his book was about.

I wanted to say no, but the Lord started pestering me about it. "You need to take Jonathan's book to Steve." I spent a lot of time in prayer about it because I never wanted people to think I was in ministry to advance my own interests or the interests of friends. Finally, confident that the Lord was in it, I e-mailed Steve the following message:

> Hi Steve,
>
> I am sorry I haven't kept in better contact, but I have been praying for you. You are someone I pray for a lot so you are being held up even when you do not know.
>
> Since you have known me for a while you know I usually do not ask for favors or anything. I do my own thing and God takes care of me. This, however, seems to be for two people.
>
> Well it is a long story but during my travels last year I met someone at an airport and it is an unusual story. Rather than go through all of it I will just give you the highlights. My flight got cancelled so I had to take the next flight out (my sister is very sick), and at the layover in North Carolina the Lord stirred my gift and I had to talk to a guy. It was somewhat strange since by the man's appearance he was Jewish. I started a casual conversation still "testing my gift" to see if I was supposed to talk to him. As we talked "it" came out and the guy was speechless.

As it turns out his name is Jonathan Cahn. He has a weekly radio show (*Two Nice Jewish Boys*) and it has been on the air for over 20 years. We were ready to board, so he asked if we could meet in the air to discuss everything more in-depth. As it came out in our meeting on the plane, he was just finishing a prophetic book to the nation (for believer and unbeliever) and was on his way to meet someone who was interested in representing him in Dallas. He was praying that God would have His way with the project and was asking the Lord for guidance in the airport. As he opened his eyes from praying I was next to him so he literally got an answer right away. He was on his way to give them the go ahead on the project. The people in Dallas were waiting on him because they were excited about his project. They said it could be a possible second *Da Vinci Code* book. In view of the word he got through me he put everything on hold to wait for God's leading.

As Jonathan has shared with me since our meeting, he finished the book a few days before I met him and I literally intercepted him to change his plans. It was two days before he told the people in Dallas that it was ready but he did not give them a verbal commitment yet. It was one day before that he had a heavy burden to pray for the Lord's will and to have His way with the book.

As I have been praying with Jonathan and on my own I felt I should contact you about this. I mentioned your name to Jonathan (I hope you don't mind) and he was excited about it. Maybe this can be a blessing for both of you? Jonathan wrote down the word he got, and some of it was something about

> being monumental. He will write a few books. Steve, I feel something is up with this so pray about it.
>
> Blessings!
>
> *Hubie*

Steve's reply came fairly quickly:

> Hubie: this is an interesting story. I can't tell if this Jewish man is a believer or not. You're not real clear on what the book is about. The *DaVinci Code* sold well but was heretical. Not sure how his book is like it. But we'd like to see it. Can you e-mail it to me?
>
> *Steve*

I put Steve in touch with Jonathan, and as the two began to talk, I felt more at ease. Yes indeed, God was in this.

As Jonathan was editing the book, he sent me part of the second chapter. It was the only part of the book I saw before its publication. Jonathan had written it before we met. In this fictional account the main character, Nouriel, sat down in a public place only to discover a man called "the prophet" sitting to his left, just as I had been sitting on Jonathan's left that day in the airport. The prophet then initiated a conversation with Nouriel, just as I had with Jonathan. The prophet then gave Nouriel a prophetic word that would lead him to write a book to bring a prophetic message to America, just as I had given Jonathan a prophetic word that would lead to the publication of *The Harbinger*, which is a prophetic word to America. I remember telling Jonathan: "You're going to write a book that will change the way people think."

The story was fictional but prophetic, and I found it pretty remarkable that Jonathan had written it before meeting me. Jonathan also sent me a prophecy from a guy in South

America that said basically the same thing I had said but using different words. "Lord, what are You doing in all this?" I wondered. I pondered the connection God had made between us at the airport and how He literally changed the weather and my flight to put us on the same airplane. Like the conductor of an orchestra He brings everything to pass at the right time. Still, it never occurred to me that the unfolding situation would change the course of my life.

After introducing Jonathan to Steve, I thought my assignment was over. My family and I started attending Jonathan's church every month or so and found his teaching phenomenal. The Lord also led me to minister to people when I was there, and I made sure to clear it with Jonathan. "I shared some words from the Lord with a few people," I said to him. "Do you mind?"

"Mind?" he said. "I'll give you the keys to lock up!"

Over the months we prayed with Jonathan and he would tell me, "The book is coming along." *The Harbinger* was published the following year on David Tyree's birthday, in a Holy Spirit coincidence. The week of its release, it became a national best seller. This was almost unheard of since Jonathan was not widely known, and *The Harbinger* was his first book. God was obviously highlighting the book's message supernaturally. Jonathan began to appear on television shows—Pat Robertson, Sid Roth, Jim Bakker—and the publisher told the story of our airport meeting and how God had superintended the book's publication. For my part, I hadn't even read the book before it came out and was very much hidden from sight, which is exactly where I wanted to be.

Charisma magazine then published an article about "the story behind the story of *The Harbinger*," and Jonathan started talking about it more publicly. "I'm telling everyone about you," he told me one day.

"Do you have to?" I asked. The level of publicity was growing uncomfortable to me. I was accustomed to listening to the Lord, ministering obediently, and retreating into private life as an accountant, father, and husband. I had no taste for the limelight. But things kept pushing my name out there.

Jonathan put the story in *The Harbinger Companion*, and Charisma House asked me to do an on-camera interview for *The Harbinger Decoded* DVD they were making. The Lord told me to say yes, and after we finished taping the interview, He began pointing out everyone on the set to whom I needed to minister.

That guy... that girl... that guy.

People were crying and weeping under the Holy Spirit's power. Even the guy running the camera had tears in his eyes. I went home stunned and more than a little afraid of what was happening.

The DVD sold out the first day. One day while flipping channels I saw a familiar face on a Christian network—my own. I immediately called Charisma House's publicity guy.

"What is this about?" I asked, genuinely perturbed.

"There's a *Harbinger Decoded* infomercial," he said. "It'll be in constant rotation from now to December."

"Yeah, but I don't want to be on TV," I said. "I didn't know they were going to air it. I just thought people would buy the DVD."

The man started laughing. I'll never forget the chill it sent up my spine.

"You can't stop it, Hubie," he said. "Quit trying."

I got so scared I actually turned white. An assignment was upon me that went way beyond my comfort level. Had

I known that sharing God's messages with people around me would lead to this, I might have tried harder to get out of those assignments. I never wanted a visible platform for ministry. I felt ill-equipped to handle it. I knew I was just a middle-aged accountant with nothing special to set me apart. "God, can't You make this go away?" I asked.

Still, I was thankful for the seasons of preparation that had molded Vicki and me for this new season. My main concern was, and is, that I don't want to mess things up. I can't imagine hurting my family or, worse, making a mockery of God. Of all the concerns that pass through my mind, that one bothers me the most.

But God continued moving quickly.

Presidential Breakfast

I did notice that the gift was operating in a more refined way over time. When I spoke to the head of a Christian television station and shared a word with him, he said the word included details from a dream God had given him. Other people described the words God gave them as intricate, detailed, and descriptive. One woman said it was like a crumb on a plate.

I also discovered that my gift works differently from the gifts of other prophetic people. Some know exactly what they are going to say before they deliver the message. Some see a picture or watch a scene as if they were watching television. Others see and read words as if they were reading a book or a newspaper article. For me, I see nothing and have no idea what I'm going to say. All I do is tap the person on the shoulder, open my mouth, and words start to flow out. I don't try to think about or listen to the words coming out of my mouth because if I do that, the flow will be interrupted.

A couple of times in the beginning I tried to listen, and the flow stopped. Maybe God in His wisdom designed the gift to work that way through me because if I knew in advance, I might think about it and back out. I am reminded of the prophecy Samuel gave to Saul when he was anointed to become king over Israel: "And the Spirit of the LORD will come upon you, and you will prophesy with them. And you will be turned into another man" (1 Sam. 10:6). That's how I feel when I prophesy—like another man, overcome by the Spirit for those moments.

And the Lord kept giving me assignments. Jonathan invited me to attend the Presidential Inaugural Prayer Breakfast he was speaking at in Washington, DC. I had friends in the area I wanted to visit as well, so I drove down. But instead of sitting and enjoying the meeting, the Lord had me ministering the whole time.

It started on my way to the bathroom. At a table near the door the Lord impressed on me, "You need to talk to that guy."

"I need to go to the bathroom," I replied. "I'll do it when I come back."

When I returned, the guy was staring at me as I came in. I went straight to him and shook his hand. "My name is Hubie, and I have something to tell you," I said. The word came out while we were holding hands in a hand-shaking pose. The next thing I knew he was weeping so much that he pulled me toward him and buried his head in my chest. It turned out he was going through a divorce and had issues with the church he led. The Lord graciously shed light on his situation and gave him hope.

I headed toward my seat, and the Lord pointed out

another guy on the way. I introduced myself and shared a word with him. Then the Lord sent me somewhere else, literally guiding me from table to table. It felt like work. One person after another I tapped on the shoulder, introduced myself, and shared whatever the Lord put in my mouth. Some of them couldn't hear me, so I brought them to the foyer just outside the triple doors.

Most were cautious, as you would expect. They would squint at me, trying to figure out who I was and why I had pulled them aside. When they heard the word, their eyes would get a little bigger, and most of the time tears would come streaming down their faces. Peace and satisfaction seemed to envelop them. Some would hug me or grip my shoulder. All were so thankful. I felt incredibly privileged to watch God at work, freeing people from the bondages of uncertainty and hopelessness.

I heard nothing of what Jonathan shared, though later I learned that the video of his message had gone viral. Toward the end of the meeting I saw a guy down on one knee. The Lord sent me to him, and I knelt down beside him. He looked up and said, "If you've got something, tell me. The Lord told me you were coming over."

I shared the word with him as he gripped my hand firmly.

"Thank you," he said. "Thank you."

"You good?" I asked.

"I'm good," he said. "Thank you. I appreciate you talking to me."

That was the last one. The Lord released me to return to my table.

"Where were you?" a friend asked.

"Working the room," I said.

When Jonathan found out I had been busy the whole time, he thought it was hysterical.

"I can't take you anywhere," he said. "You don't get a moment to relax."

From that point on, whenever the Lord sends me somewhere, I expect Him to use me in the gift. I know He has an agenda for me. Sometimes it means giving words to people in power like US congressmen, ministry leaders, and others in various fields. One time I shared a word from the Lord with a professional skateboarder who was so stunned he hugged me and started crying, soaking my shirt in snot and tears.

Still, it was a big adjustment going from behind the scenes to out in the open. Life became surreal at times, but Vicki and I felt steady because God had taken us through seasons of trials and character development to equip us. It was His work, not ours, and obedience was the only response we could have. Having walked with God so long, we couldn't imagine any other way.

Every day we ask ourselves, "Where is God leading us next?" As long as He is leading, we are determined to keep growing in Him. That means holding on to the prophetic principles and important lessons He has given us along the way. I will share those in the final chapter.

Chapter 10

PRINCIPLES FOR PROPHESYING

When we begin operating in our spiritual gifts, it requires a great deal of learning and stretching. That doesn't just happen—it takes effort on our part. As I have sought to learn more about my gift and serve more faithfully in it, I have seen God increase it in many ways. I want to encourage you to take the same approach. Faithfulness means partnering with the Holy Spirit and carrying your end of the commitment. Let me share some of the most important principles I have discovered while growing in the prophetic gift.

Don't Be Afraid

The first principle—don't fear—is the one that looms largest for me. Though I know prophecy produces much good, having the gift of prophecy is scary for me. I feel like I am walking on water whenever I have to tap someone on the shoulder to give him a word. I am tempted with all kinds of fear—fear of rejection, fear of embarrassment, fear of getting in trouble, and fear of making a mistake. I never know how people will react or interpret the words God gives them. I do not want to lead people down the wrong path. All these thoughts cross my mind as I am about to prophesy.

Every time it happens, I have to choose not to allow these fears to overcome me. I remember that God is in control and is with me at all times. In my weakness He is strong. When I open my mouth to speak, I know it is His Spirit speaking through me and not my own voice—His power, not mine. I'm just the instrument He's using. If I make a mistake with good intentions, God will mercifully correct my course. That gives me great comfort.

I have found that the key to confronting fear is to acknowledge it, then say no, and move on with what God tells you to do. There's no use denying that fear is there, but we must deny fear any power in that moment. I remind myself that God qualifies those He calls. His strength is made perfect in our weakness. We do our part, but He is responsible for the outcome. I get great encouragement and boldness from reading the Word. Jesus said:

> But when you are arrested and stand trial, don't worry in advance about what to say. Just say what God tells you at that time, for it is not you who will be speaking, but the Holy Spirit.
>
> —MARK 13:11, NLT

God told Joshua:

> Have not I commanded you? Be strong and courageous. Do not be afraid or dismayed, for the LORD your God is with you wherever you go.
>
> —JOSHUA 1:9

The prophet Isaiah spoke for God when he wrote:

> Do not fear, for I am with you; do not be dismayed, for I am your God. I will strengthen you, I will help you, yes, I will uphold you with My righteous right hand.
>
> —Isaiah 41:10

Paul reminded Timothy to stir up the gift of God that was within him, "for God has not given us a spirit of fear, but of power and of love and of a sound mind" (2 Tim. 1:7, NKJV). In these verses we are commanded to use our gifts and not to give any place to fear. This means that obedience is the eager, active exercise of our spiritual gifts in total obedience, knowing that God will not let us down. In the Book of Acts I see over and over again how Jesus's followers were obedient and humble. Fear did not factor into their decisions. They knew God was kind and merciful and would not lead them into assignments only to leave them stranded.

I want to be candid and tell you that though it is a great privilege to watch God work through this gift, I do not like to prophesy to people. I only accept the assignments because they benefit the body of Christ. There is no other reason. So I work hard to cultivate a fear of God that is greater than my fear of people. I make sure I fear disobeying Him more than I fear any particular situation. This kind of righteous fear of God keeps me on track. And my natural reluctance actually serves as my "check" to prevent pride and overconfidence from creeping into my motives.

Overcoming fear is worth it. The more I serve God, the more I see how every single thing He tells me to do has purpose and significance. It may not make sense or seem important at the time, but God knows the eventual impact. Prophesying to David Tyree is one example. I had no idea the word I shared was pointing to a famous catch he would make in the Super Bowl. I didn't know our friendship would redirect our lives and ministry.

The frightening truth is that I could have refused to call David Tyree. Would the word still have gotten to him? Yes, I believe so—through someone else. In other words, when you refuse to take an assignment, you are really saying no to the blessing of participating with the Holy Spirit in His work today. You are subtracting yourself from the kingdom equation. My hunch is that a lot of people chicken out because they are scared to make a mistake or deal with perceived negative consequences. Their thoughts are entirely on themselves, not on the kingdom work. They are self-focused, and their fear of people has outgrown their fear of God. That's a terrible situation.

For my part, I don't want to stand before God and see how many times I missed assignments because my fear of man was greater than my faith in God. Exercising our spiritual gifts is not optional; it's a command. That should make us tremble—and obey.

SIFT THE STIRRING

It might seem like I resist or complain often when the Lord directs me to talk with someone, but some of that is my way of testing the impulse. When I feel the stirring in my stomach to speak to someone, I don't run over to that person right away. I wait to see if the stirring continues, because I want to be absolutely sure it is God directing me.

While waiting, I examine myself to make sure I am in right standing with God and that I don't have wrong motives in my heart concerning what I am about to do. (See 2 Corinthians 13:5.) I never skip this very important step. Jeremiah 18:3–4 tells the story of the potter who had to remake the vessel because he noticed an imperfection. Philippians 1:6 speaks of God having begun a good work in us to complete it until the day of Jesus Christ. These verses confirm that each of us is still being molded and perfected and that there is room for error. None of us should become prideful and think that we are always right. Psalm 19:12–14 puts it so well:

> Who can understand his errors? Cleanse me from secret faults. Keep back Your servant also from presumptuous sins; may they not rule over me. Then I will be upright and innocent from great transgression. Let the words of my mouth and the meditation of my heart be acceptable in Your sight, O Lord, my strength and my Redeemer.

Before sharing a word with someone, it's OK to sift it for a moment. God allows time for this. Check your motives. Pray and ask the Lord for a clean heart, to keep you from "presumptuous sins," and that the words of your mouth would be acceptable in His sight.

Establish Boundaries

When God accelerated the use of my gift, Vicki had a number of different reactions. First, she was happy and relieved to see her husband coming along in his walk with God. Recall that when we were first married, neither of us was walking with the Lord. When we came back to church, Vicki often asked God, "Is Hubie going to have the same love and passion and desire to serve You that I do?" Seeing me grow in the Lord and be used by Him was a big relief for her. It also fulfilled her to see me becoming the head of household and leading our family in a godly way.

But when I started prophesying more frequently, including to women, Vicki was tempted to feel threatened, jealous, and insecure. I was spending a lot of time on ministry trips with people she barely knew, and of course it wasn't a welcome sight to see me interacting with women who were attractive and single. Even less did she like the idea of women calling or texting me later with follow-up questions.

I mentioned earlier some of the boundaries we established: I don't minister to people one-on-one in private. I don't hug women if I can help it, and I cut communication short if they later try to text or call me. I'm not saying everyone has wrong motives, but Vicki and I are determined to go the extra mile to protect our marriage and ministry from even a hint of scandal. I told Vicki when we got married, "We're doing this once." I meant it then, and I mean it now.

We also established an open text and e-mail policy. Vicki is free to pick up my phone at any time and read my texts and e-mails. A couple of times she has done this and said, "Ugh, I wish I hadn't read that," because people text me all sorts of issues they are having. Again, I rarely call people back or continue a conversation beyond what is necessary. And Vicki can see whatever communication I have with them. I encourage you, go to great lengths to protect your marriage and family relationships. Set boundaries further out than they need to be so everyone knows you are serious about having integrity and protecting the most important relationships in your life.

DON'T CHASE PROPHECY

Some people rely on prophecy too much. They like the "rush" of hearing from God. They want a "fresh word" every day. That is not the way God designed us to live. The Bible says we walk by faith, not by sight (2 Cor. 5:7). Prophetic words can give us something to hold on to, but they are not our daily bread.

When people obsess about the prophetic gift and seek new words all the time, it starts to distort the precious relationship Jesus wants to have with them. They think they can't hear God for themselves. By chasing prophecy, they cut themselves off from personal contact with God. Jesus said, "My sheep hear My voice" (John 10:27). That's a promise for each one of us, not just the prophetically gifted. We all must hear from God for ourselves. Occasionally He will speak through other people, but that is the exception, not the rule. If you are not hearing from God in daily prayer times and in reading the Word, a prophecy will steer you in a certain direction, but how will you really know it is accurate? How can you test it as Scripture says to do?

Some people call and text me for months after I meet them. These "prophecy groupies" just want a new word and think that sooner or later I will wear down and give them one. They have a total misunderstanding of how the gifts work. Prophesying is not under my control. Peter said, "No prophecy of Scripture comes from someone's own interpretation. For no prophecy was ever produced by the will of man, but men spoke from God as they were carried along by the Holy Spirit" (2 Pet. 1:20–21, ESV). I have never given anybody a word that I willed to happen; it all comes from God. I want to be kind to people who are desperate for God, but also say, "I'm glad you had a divine encounter, but you need to seek God on your own through the Word and in prayer. Do those things and see what happens."

If you are relying on a prophet, pastor, elder, deacon, counselor, or anyone else to give you regular supernatural direction, you are probably in an unhealthy situation. Vicki and I know this from experience. I do not think God sends prophets to pour into the same people over and over again. In fact, I am more impacted when I get a word from someone I don't know and who couldn't possibly know details about my life. That's when I really sense that God knows my address and cares about my circumstance.

On the other side, if you are a prophetic person, you must not become addicted to or enamored of giving words to people. If your motivation is wrong, you can easily start to draw people unto yourself instead of to Jesus. Some prophetic people I know feel great pressure to perform. The temptation to perform came to us when God began releasing me to prophesy more. People at church would be friendly with Vicki because they wanted to get to me. Some would take pictures with her. Eventually we realized what was happening and deliberately tried to stay out of sight. I do not like the idea of being treated like a celebrity.

I want to warn those of you who are prophetically gifted: If you act the part of the celebrity prophet, it will draw people to you. And it will pollute the exercise of your gift and eventually do as much harm as the good that God intended.

The solution to all of this, as with everything, is love. When we love people with God's love, we don't want to use them for our own selfish purposes. We don't try to draw attention to ourselves. And on the other side we don't resent people for "chasing a word." Loving people without expecting anything in return, and without expecting them to be fully mature, opens the way to minister to them freely. Pure motivation means wanting to give people the same love we received from God. God's focus is always on relationship with Him, not on spiritual gifts, acts, and accomplishments. Those are just the means to an end. Study 1 Corinthians 12–14 to see how critical love is to the proper functioning of the spiritual gifts. Let love purify your motivation and keep your heart right before God and people as you prophesy.

Let It Unfold

Many prophecies give general direction but not as much detail as we would like. I believe this is because God wants to give us just enough hope to keep us moving in the right direction. It is not our job to figure it out. But most people's tendency—and Vicki and I have been guilty of this many times—is to interpret a word immediately and try to fit it into their present circumstances. This leads away from hope and toward doubt, discouragement, and despair. We have to keep in mind that God works on a much longer time frame than we do. He exists outside of time. When He tells you something prophetically, you usually will have no idea if it will happen when you are younger or older.

For example, it was prophesied to me when I was in my late twenties that I would be handling money for a lot of people, that they would come to me for counsel, and that I wouldn't have to worry financially. I am now almost fifty years old and am just starting to see what that word means. Was it accurate? Yes. Has it happened? Some of it. But I well remember trying to make decisions based on that word in my thirties and forties and wondering why it made no sense. Instead of letting the prophecy unfold in God's timing, I was trying to help God get us there.

God uses prophecy to inform His children of things that are yet to come so that we will have hope while we wait and will be attentive to the signs when they start appearing. Jesus cautioned us many times to stay alert, stay awake, not to get drowsy in our walk with Him. Prophecy helps us to stay alert, stay excited, and stay engaged in the work while we wait for promised things to come to pass. Now when Vicki and I receive a word, we say, "Thank You, Lord. We will hold on to that and remember it." When it starts to unfold, we say, "The signs are starting to show up. Something must be happening." We are prepared and openhearted because of the prophecy.

Let me address one more thing here: If you have received and acted on a false prophecy, don't get stuck in regret. The Bible says we see in part and we know in part (1 Cor. 13:9, 12). Prophecy is not going to be perfect, and God does not want us to get bogged down in bitterness. The important thing is to remain sincere and loving toward God and people, open to correction, and not afraid of moving in the spiritual gifts. Simply repent to the Lord, forgive yourself, and forgive the person who gave the false prophecy. Then resist the temptation to take offense.

If you have suffered hurt and loss, you may want to seek help for healing as Vicki and I did after our experience. Give yourself time, and step away from ministry for a season if the Lord leads you to. There's no need to feel guilty about taking time to heal. Your heavenly Father loves you too much to allow you to stay wounded.

When you receive a prophecy, pray about it and allow the Holy Spirit to help you discern whether to receive or reject it. Then, unless the prophecy contains detailed, specific instructions or direction regarding a situation you know requires immediate action, allow the events to unfold. Resist the temptation or pressure to interpret it right away or to make things happen. God already has the plan laid out, and your job is to walk in it one step at a time, whether or not you understand it.

Go With the Flow

As you move in the gifts and surrender yourself to God, He may use your time in ways that make no sense to you. My advice: Deal with it. Give up your schedule.

I was always taught to have goals in life. I had things I wanted to achieve by a certain age, places I wanted to go, goals for my family, goals for my hobbies, goals for work, goals for finances, goals for friendships.

All those goals have gone away. Over time I have surrendered them to the Lord. Even my daily schedule is His. I start each day by surrendering it to Him. My vision is to do what God wants me to do and go where God wants me to go. So when I wake up, I pray in my heart, "I have things in mind that I plan to do, but that's all secondary. I will do whatever You want me to do and go wherever You lead me."

Vicki likes to know where I am, so the fact that I did not know frustrated her. I would say, "I think I'm going to be here or there, but I'm not sure." I understand how that exasperated her, but God was training me to let Him order my day, to make all my plans tentative. The apostle James said as much:

> Come now, you who say, "Today or tomorrow we will go to such and such a city, spend a year there, buy and sell, and make a profit"; whereas you do not know what will happen tomorrow. For what is your life? It is even a vapor that appears for a little time and then vanishes away. Instead you ought to say, "If the Lord wills, we shall live and do this

> or that." But now you boast in your arrogance. All such boasting is evil.
>
> —JAMES 4:13–16, NKJV

God is the author of time and is trustworthy to plan your calendar. His daily agenda should be your only agenda—no more, no less. You might need to change your paradigm, because life is not about how to fit God into our day, but about allowing God to fill and order our days. Vicki and I learned this repeatedly when hosting worship gatherings in our home. Once ministry began, we didn't know when it would end. When God sent people to our home, we didn't feel right saying, "It's eleven o'clock. Time for everyone to leave." How many ministry opportunities would we have missed?

When I began to travel for ministry, God did the same thing. One time I was invited to extend a ministry trip in Florida, even though I really wanted to go home. Vicki prayed about it, and the Holy Spirit said, "Tell Hubie to go to Fort Lauderdale and await further instructions." We didn't know anything more than that. So I obeyed, and God opened doors to fruitful ministry there.

I have seen God open doors so many times that by now I'm afraid to say no to Him. I know He always has a purpose for telling me to speak to someone or go somewhere. I am getting better at trusting that He will give me time to rest or will impart supernatural strength if I am feeling weak. A good example is the divine appointment with Jonathan Cahn at the Charlotte airport. I was tired and cranky, but my obedience changed both our lives and set the course for publication of *The Harbinger*.

Yes, it's scary to call a client some days and say, "I can't come in like we planned. Something has come up." But I have placed my trust in God. If He makes me cancel meetings, I know it's for a good purpose. If He messes with my schedule, it's a good thing, not a bad thing. He will do the same for you—prying your fingers off the steering wheel of your life and forcing you to give up your petty sense of control. When you become willing to accept the unknown, your gift will operate much more freely.

In this process Vicki has discovered the ministry of waiting. When I minister now at church services or meetings, it can go on for hours. That doesn't faze her anymore. In fact, sometimes Vicki will know before I do that there is more ministry to be done. I'll say, "I'm ready to go." Vicki will laugh, poke me in the arm, and say almost jokingly, "You think we're going home now? Oh, really?" Sure enough, something will happen and the ministry will continue. My daughter Sara does the same thing to me. Vicki even senses that certain days will be about ministry, not working my regular job. In the morning she will say something like, "So, you're going to be working today, huh?" Then she'll laugh, and I know God has something different in store.

We have come a long way in being flexible with our time. We used to compartmentalize it, saying, "When we're on vacation, we're on vacation, period. No ministry." That just doesn't work. God's work is who we are and part of everything we do. Our time is not our own, and there is no convenient or perfect time to do His will. We no longer plan our vacations, because God already has the plans and He lets us know where to go. He even sets up all the details so we walk in the path He's prepared.

You can't be a control freak and walk obediently with the Lord. Put aside your own agenda, and make Him the Lord of your schedule.

STAY CLEAN BY FORGIVING

It's amazing how long we carry some scars. A memory from my childhood in Texas always stung me. My mother was faithfully doing whatever she could to bring God into our lives. One Sunday one of us was sick, so we stayed home from church. Mom went to the kitchen, got some grape juice from the fridge and crackers from the pantry, and brought them to her bedroom. Then she brought out her treasured Bible, large and white with elaborate pictures.

She was smiling with joy as she brought it into room and opened it to the Gospel of Matthew. She placed the Bible on her bed, and we each got up to read as the priests did at Sunday Mass. After reading, we each stood in front of the Bible and said what we thought the scripture meant. Then we had confession and Communion. It was a lot more interesting and fun to us than regular church. After our homemade service, we danced, sang, and spent time together. It was a special day.

The next Sunday we went back to church, and my mother met with the priest afterward. She came back to us in tears. That night after dinner she called us to the kitchen table and told us we would not be returning to that church. The priest had severely chastised her about the service we held at home, saying we made a mockery of the church and of God and had committed a mortal sin. We all bowed our heads and each asked God to forgive us for what we had done.

We kids were confused. How could something so fun be so bad? I did not know it, but the episode left a tremendous scar on my life.

Decades later I went to visit dear friends of mine, Rena and Rene Cruz, and while I was at their house, they felt the need to pray for me. Suddenly they both asked about my childhood, and in my answer the church incident came up, replaying vividly in my mind. I recalled the sunlight coming through the window, the color of the floor, and what we were all wearing. I didn't even know I remembered all those details. Then I felt the need to forgive the priest for what he did to us. It was an intense prayer session. Apparently I had hidden bitterness in my heart for all that time. As I forgave the priest, God's peace covered me, and a weight was lifted. Praise God! It felt so good.

To seal it, God had a special gift for me. A couple of years later I went to Texas to visit my mother's side of the family. A relative, who was very dear to me, said she had something for me. She went into the other room and emerged with my mother's Bible, the one we had used in the home church service.

"I am sure she would want you to have it," she said.

For me, it was more than a cherished heirloom—it was a physical reminder that God had been pleased with us that day and that I could walk in total forgiveness and freedom. That's a principle for each one of us: Keep your heart clean. Let God heal those areas of bitterness and brokenness over time. Don't let them become hindrances to His present work in and through your life.

Get a Mentor

Having a mentor has done wonders for my growth in prophetic ministry. I have someone to answer my questions, give counsel, offer encouragement, and just plain enjoy friendship with. If you have a prophetic call on your life, pray for God to give you a mentor to whom you can be accountable, someone who can help you understand your gift and how to use it.

LET YOUR MINISTRY GROW AND BE UNIQUE

I believe each person's spiritual gifts manifest uniquely through his or her personality, strengths, and calling in Christ. There are general principles but no cookie-cutter approach to our gifts. I encourage you to grow in your unique way. Don't be afraid if God does things differently with you than with others. His expression of love through your personality and relationships and gifts and talents will be distinct and wonderful. Embrace the differences; learn from them. Grow in the adventure of discovering who God has made you to be.

Let me share some observations I have made about my own prophetic calling that I hope will encourage you to appreciate the distinctive, specific calling God has given you:

- The Lord often sends me to give a word to someone right before a big change or breakthrough in their lives. I don't know why, but I have observed that pattern.
- The Lord often puts me backstage or in places where leaders gather so I can speak His words to them. Many of these people are on the road all the time, playing music or ministering, and they don't get ministered to much. They are always so receptive and appreciative of hearing from the Lord.
- I minister to everybody, not just those in positions of power. The few times I have been on Christian television, I ministered to the staff,

the hair dresser, the camera operators, and so on. When I was backstage for one show, they had to come find me because I was ministering to a behind-the-scenes worker and almost missed my cue. "Just get out there!" they said and virtually shoved me through the door onto the set. That explains why I look so disoriented in those first few seconds.

- The operation of the gift greatly disoriented me at first. At times it seemed to flare up beyond my control wherever I went—in parking lots, on vacations, at kids' birthday parties. For a time I felt I lost my identity and couldn't go anywhere safely. It took time and practice to learn to manage the spirit of prophecy.

  That included dealing with the heightened sensitivity to spiritual environments. As God used me more and more, I would walk into places and feel the fear, unrest, paranoia, pride, and greed residing in people there. In my profession the only concern is money, so there's a lot of darkness. It has been difficult to tolerate those environments in my working life.

- I now know that the Lord will give the same word a second time if the person did not catch it the first time. When God gives me a word, it comes in a flow, and I can stay in that flow a little while if the person needs to hear parts of it again or wants clarity. When the word finishes, it goes into pause mode, and I ask the person, "Did you get it?" If they didn't get it, the flow restarts and sometimes comes in more detail. But in general I cannot turn the flow on or off like a light switch. If someone says, "I got it," then the flow stops and I can't bring it back.

- The Lord will use visuals to help get His message across. I find myself using cups, cell phones, or nearby available objects to demonstrate in a visual way what the word is saying. A certain configuration or relationship or sequence can help to illuminate the word. I might draw something on paper or diagram it invisibly on my hand. Visuals stick in the memory.

  I am told that when speaking a word, I make emphatic gestures with my hands. That's funny because I always made fun of people who used their hands to speak. Now I am one of them. Jonathan Cahn has told me that sometimes I stop for a moment as if the Lord is hunting down the right word on my "hard drive" to use. Once He finds it, I start again. Those are some peculiarities I have noticed as I learn about how this gift operates in me.

- Your gift can expand and improve. When I came back from receiving ministry at Bethel Church in Redding, California, my gift became noticeably stronger. I can look at photographs and see into people's lives. That's a long way from where I started. I used to get intimidated when people stuck recorders or iPhones in my face to record what I said, or started writing words down as I spoke them. I felt distracted or that it was disrespectful. Now it's no big deal.

I would encourage you to go where ministry is happening and see if that has an effect on how your spiritual gift operates. Also, be open to things that initially cause you discomfort. It's part of the learning process.

- I rarely receive prophetic words these days. This has become a joke with Vicki and me. It doesn't matter who we are with or how much prophecy is flowing; I almost always get left out. For example, I was with John Paul Jackson and gave him a word. Then I asked if he had one for me. "No," he said. Thankfully, I understand my identity in Christ a lot better than before and don't need frequent prophetic affirmation. I am confident that God loves me and is with me no matter what.

- You can prophesy to your own family. It doesn't happen to us much, but now and then God does send a word to my wife through me. It can be very uncomfortable. One time we were having a heated argument late at night at a relative's house. We were trying to keep our voices down, and at some point Vicki retreated to the bathroom to cry silently into a towel. It was a really terrible night, and right in the middle of it I felt God stirring me. I could hardly believe it.

Vicki came back to bed, and I said, "God wants to tell you something." That didn't go over well because I was the last person on the planet she wanted to speak with. Reluctantly she turned to me, and the flow began. It was a very important word for our future. Thankfully Vicki recognizes that there's a certain look I have when the gift operates. That helps us to put other things aside, but it can be hard to switch gears.

Even stranger, it is possible to prophesy to yourself. Vicki has seen me on numerous occasions prophesying over a friend or loved one when suddenly the Holy Spirit turns His attention to me. Without knowing what I'm doing, I tug my own shirt and say, "For this one here..." And out comes the word. It's a good thing Vicki hears it because I never do, even though the word is for me. Vicki finds this hilarious.

- Prophetic ministry is really draining. Something about the flow of the Spirit through me just wears me out. It doesn't matter if it's one person or fifty whom I minister to. I still feel the same the next day. My knees get weak and I have to budget recovery time for my mind and body.
- You would think that prophecy has become part of my personal identity, but the truth is that I would not be disappointed if the gift stopped operating, unless stopping hurt the body of Christ. As long as I'm in close

> relationship with God all day, I'm fine with Him using me prophetically or not. I am who I am. It doesn't affect the important things in life.

Facebook Prophesying

I'll end with a story. Vicki and I don't watch much TV, but one night we were watching *Hell's Kitchen* with Chef Gordon Ramsay. One of the contestants, Elise Wims (who was playing the villain), was a loud-mouthed girl with a bad attitude. She made it into the top three, which was really an accomplishment. Something about the woman stuck with me, so I found her on Facebook, and God had me send her a word. There was no reply. A couple of weeks later at the Lord's prompting I sent her another one. Again, no reply.

"That's it," I told Vicki. "I'm done with that. I don't want to be accused of stalking." But a couple of weeks later the Lord was emphatic: "Go look at her photos on Facebook." There I saw a picture of Elise with a woman I had never seen. "You need to tell that woman something," the Lord said, indicating the other woman in the photo. The post gave no indication who she was. So I posted a comment asking, "Who is the woman with you in this photo?" The daughter of the woman replied, "None of your business."

But the Lord kept on me, so I typed up the word and sent it to Elise. A couple of days later she started to follow me on Facebook, then sent a message saying, "Hi. Nice to meet you. I know you're legit." She included her phone number and asked me to call her. Vicki and I talked about it and felt it was right, so I did.

"I really wanted to tell you what happened," she said when

I called her. Her voice grew more emotional over the course of the conversation. "The woman in the photo is a relative. You sent her this word and you don't know who she is. I read it over the phone to her and she started crying. She demanded I go to her house immediately because she was so overcome, so I printed it out and took it to her."

This woman had been praying for some specific things, and the Lord gave her answers about them and about questions from her past. There was no way I could have known them. She was a complete stranger to me. I had only seen her photo on Facebook.

Elise has become a family friend, and we have had the privilege of helping her through some life struggles. She has spent time in our home and told us many times that she doesn't know where she would be without us. The Lord clearly singled her out for ministry and gave us the honor of being His vessels. She has also poured into my life. She inspired me to cook again, and I love cooking for my family now.

Through all the crazy and marvelous things God has done, I am most thankful that there has been fruit in people's lives. Bearing fruit brings glory to God, and that is the purpose of all creation. I want to emphasize again how unlikely I feel to be used in this spiritual gift and how I believe it is a sure promise that God will use each of us. After all, I was in my forties when the gift first began manifesting, and I did not see it coming.

I have come to believe that every believer has one or more spiritual gifts, and none of us really know what the Lord has planned for our lives until it starts to unfold. If you have yet to discover your spiritual gifts, or don't know how or where to start using them, just be obedient where you are. God has a purpose in everything, even the smallest assignments. He takes time to build a foundation so our work will be sure and stable. Don't disqualify yourself because of age or origin or because it seems to be taking so long. Jesus needed just three years to start and finish His ministry. Think of what the Lord can do with the years He has given you.

Though Vicki and I have been part of some exciting things the Lord has done, in some ways we haven't changed at all. I'm still an accountant. I drive into New York City a couple of times a week, park near the Lincoln Tunnel, and work for my clients there. If people recognize me, they think I'm that intellectual Japanese professor on science shows on TV. They ask for autographs and are disappointed when they realize I'm not him. Vicki and I are busy raising our kids and trying to hear and obey God as best we can. Our lives are in some ways radically normal.

If God will use people like us, He is eager to use you too. In His own unique and unpredictable way, He will use your life to tell tales worth sharing—and I look forward to hearing those someday. May God bless you now as you follow Him in the adventure ahead.